access to p

UK GOVERNMENT *and* POLITICS *in* CONTEXT

David Simpson

Series Editor: David Simpson

Hodder & Stoughton
A MEMBER OF THE HODDER HEADLINE GROUP

ACKNOWLEDGEMENTS

The publishers would like to thank the following for granting permission to reproduce images:

p 22: Press Association/Topham
p 43: Howard Barlow
p 86: Jan Brown Design
p 97: Popperfoto/Reuters

Order queries: please contact Bookpoint Ltd, 39 Milton Park, Abingdon, Oxon OX14 4TD. Telephone: (44) 01235 400414, Fax: (44) 01235 400454. Lines are open from 9.00 - 6.00, Monday to Saturday with a 24 hour message answering service. Email address: orders@bookpoint.co.uk

A catalogue record for this title is available from The British Library

ISBN 0 340 711345

First published 1998
Impression number 10 9 8 7 6 5 4 3 2 1
Year 2003 2002 2001 2000 1999 1998

Cover photos from The Telegraph Colour Library

Typeset by Transet Limited, Coventry, England.
Printed in Great Britain for Hodder & Stoughton Educational, a division of Hodder Headline plc, 338 Euston Road, London NW1 3BH by Redwood Books, Trowbridge, Wilts.

CONTENTS

PREFACE

A/AS Level syllabuses in Government and Politics aim to develop knowledge and understanding of the political system of the UK. They cover its local, national and European Union dimensions, and include comparative studies of aspects of other political systems, in order to ensure an understanding of the distinctive nature of the British political system. The minimum requirements for comparative study are aspects of systems with a separation of powers, how other systems protect the rights of individuals and how other electoral systems work.

Access to Politics is a series of concise topic books which cover the syllabus requirements, providing students with the necessary resources to complete the course successfully.

General advice on approaching exam questions

To achieve high grades you need to demonstrate consistency. Clearly address all parts of a question, make good use of essay plans or notes, and plan your time to cover all the questions.

Make your answers stand out from the crowd by using contemporary material to illustrate them. You should read a quality newspaper and listen to or watch appropriate programmes on radio and television.

Skills Advice

You should comprehend, synthesise and interpret political information in a variety of forms:

- Analyse and evaluate political institutions, processes and behaviour, political arguments and explanations.
- Identify parallels, connections, similarities and differences between aspects of the political systems studied.
- Select and organise relevant material to construct arguments and explanations leading to reasoned conclusions.
- Communicate the arguments with relevance, clarity and coherence, using vocabulary appropriate to the study of Government and Politics.

1

INTRODUCTION

ONE OF THE three specific comparative elements required in A/AS Level syllabuses in Government and Politics is some comparative study of aspects of systems with a **separation of powers**, in order to draw out the nature of the British system. The name most closely associated with the doctrine of the separation of powers is Charles Louis de Secondat, Baron Montesquieu, a French political philosopher of the eighteenth century. He asserted that liberty is lost if the three powers of the legislature (law-making), executive (law-application) and judiciary (law-adjudication) are not separated.

Constitutional thought in the American colonies before the creation of the Federal Constitution of 1787 reflects a number of interwoven influences at work. British thought and the pattern of British institutions inevitably provided the starting point for American development. However, although it was adapted to the American environment, the structure of British constitutional theory (in which monarch, Lords and Commons operated a complex system of checks and balances upon each other) was potentially at variance with the social structure of the colonies. Balanced constitution in Britain acknowledged the importance of monarchy and aristocracy, with their claim to the exercise of power, but the claims of the Crown in the colonies (represented by the Governor) were far greater than the prerogative powers exercised in practice by the monarch in Britain. The growing objections of the colonists to the excessive power of the governors were therefore expressed in terms of the need to maintain a proper balance in the constitution.

As the conflict deepened, the theory of the balanced constitution became irrelevant, and the separation of powers emerged as the only available basis of a constitutional government. The actual outbreak of a revolution that leaned heavily upon the relatively democratic character of the American way of life rendered the old theory of government wholly inappropriate. For a short period the pure doctrine of the separation of powers emerged in America and was incorporated in varying degrees into the institutional structure of the revolutionary State governments.

With the attainment of independence, however, those leaders in America who had allied with radical forces for the purposes of the revolution, turned back again to the old ideas of balanced government, grafting it on to the new basis of American constitutional thought to provide a new and unique combination of the separation of powers and checks and balances.

- The USA is the classic example of a presidential system of government based upon a strict application of the doctrine of the separation of powers (Chapter 3).
- This doctrine is one of the defining features of liberal democracy in the USA (Chapter 4).
- Systems of government with a separation of powers have different arrangements for dealing with the conflict between the desire that governments should be responsive to public opinion and that they should pursue policies which are wise and consistent (Chapter 5).
- The presidential system in the USA allows one party to capture the executive while the other controls the legislature, a two-party system different in nature from the British party system (Chapter 6).
- One of the arguments against a written or codified constitution for Britain is that the existing system retains the internal checks and balances that A.V. Dicey identified in the nineteenth century (Chapter 2).

2

THE BRITISH CONSTITUTION IN CONTEXT

Introduction

THIS CHAPTER WILL define a constitution, distinguishing between 'written' and 'unwritten', 'rigid' and 'flexible', federal' and 'unitary' constitutions, and it will also define devolution, considering then the case for and the case against federalism.

It will explain the 'essential principles' of the British Constitution, and it will assess the impact of membership of the European Union on it.

Finally, it will consider the case for and the case against a 'written' or codified constitution, as well as some of the broad issues that would arise if Britain were to adopt a 'written' constitution.

Key Points

- Definition of a constitution.
- 'Essential principles' of the British Constitution.
- The European Union dimension
- The case for and the case against a 'written' or codified constitution.

THE DEFINITION OF A CONSTITUTION

In the narrow, concrete sense a **constitution** is the document which contains major rules regulating a political system. However, in the broader, abstract sense it is all the rules which regulate a political system. It regulates the composition and powers of governmental institutions, and the relationships between these institutions, as well as between them and the individual citizen.

THE UNWRITTEN BRITISH CONSTITUTION

WRITTEN AND UNWRITTEN CONSTITUTIONS

The traditional terms employed to distinguish between the forms in which a constitution may be expressed are those of 'written' and 'unwritten'.

A constitution is said to be **written** when major rules of the constitution are contained in one formal document, 'The Constitution'. Nearly all constitutions are 'written'. For example, in the USA the powers and limitations of the President and his Administration are contained in Article 2 of the United States Constitution. Provisions of written constitutions may be justiciable, that is enforceable in the courts. For example, the case of Marbury v Madison in 1803 (a dispute over the appointment of judges) was fundamental in holding the United States Constitution to be justiciable. Chief Justice Marshall held that it was 'a proposition too plain to be contested that the constitution controls any legislative act repugnant to it' and asserted the right of the United States Supreme Court to strike down such legislation.

A constitution is said to be **unwritten** when there is no one document or even series of formally related documents that can be identified as 'The Constitution'. Britain, like Israel, can be said to have an unwritten constitution.

However, the distinction between written and unwritten constitutions is misleading. No constitution is entirely written in the sense that all its major rules are contained in one document or even a series of formally related documents. For example, in the USA, institutions of major constitutional significance such as Primaries (intra-party elections) are not regulated, nor even mentioned, in the US Constitution, but have evolved. At the same time, no constitution is entirely unwritten in the sense that none of its major rules are written in formal documents. Some of the major rules of the British Constitution are written in **statute law**, which is made by Parliament. For example, the Parliament Acts of 1911 and 1949, which regulate the maximum duration of Parliament and the powers of the House of Lords, are clearly part of the 'law of the constitution'.

Other major constitutional rules are contained in the **common law**, which is judge-made law that has developed over centuries. For example, the **royal prerogative**, that is, the powers legally left in the hands of the Crown, is a product of the common law. The Prime Minister is appointed and Parliament is dissolved by royal prerogative.

Britain ratified the European Convention on Human Rights in 1951, and since 1955 has accepted the right of individual petition to the European Commission on Human Rights.

Some major constitutional rules are contained in the **conventions of the constitution**, that is rules which are not law. For example, it is a convention that the monarch must assent to any bill passed by the two Houses of Parliament. Even some conventions, however, are written in the sense that they are contained in formal documents. For example, the conventions of collective responsibility and individual ministerial responsibility are contained in the Ministerial Code which has been published by the Cabinet Office since 1992 (see Chapter 5).

What Britain has is best described as a part-written but uncodified constitution.

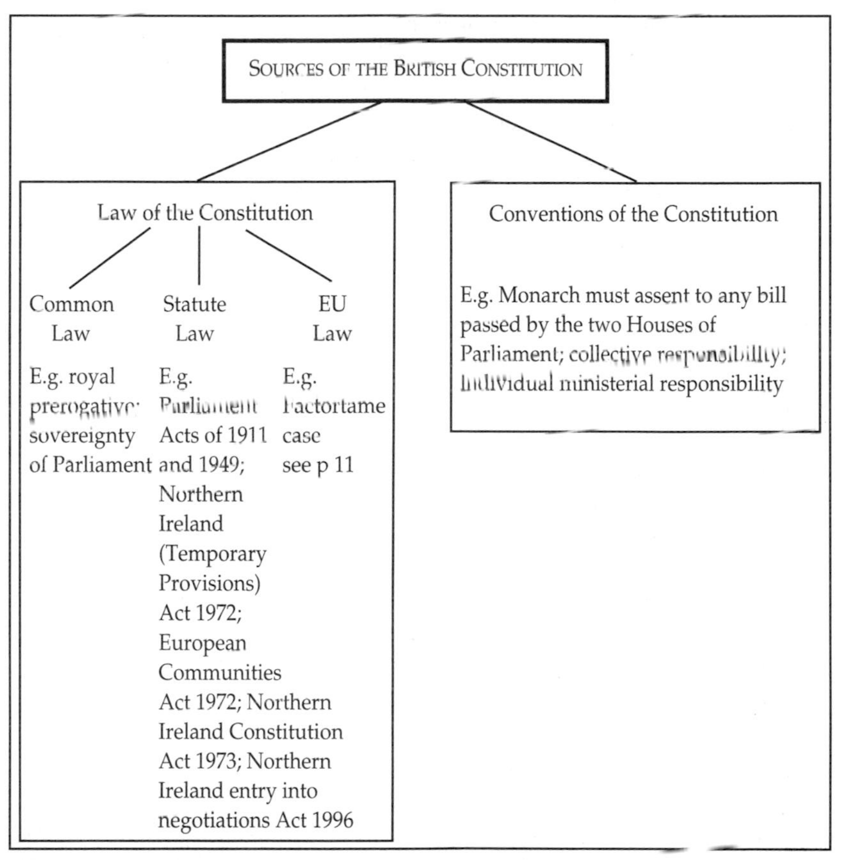

SOURCES OF THE BRITISH CONSTITUTION

THE FLEXIBLE BRITISH CONSTITUTION

Constitutions differ over the methods by which they may be changed.

RIGID AND FLEXIBLE CONSTITUTIONS

A **rigid constitution** is one which can only be amended by an extraordinary procedure. It would appear common for so-called written constitutions to have special procedures for amending their provisions. In such cases the document and its provisions are generally referred to as being entrenched. Usually, written constitutions entrench certain provisions of the constitution that are regarded as being of fundamental importance.

Many entrench all their provisions equally. For example, in the USA an amendment to the Constitution requires the approval of two-thirds of the members of each House of Congress and ratification by the legislatures in three-quarters of the states (or, alternatively, approval by a gathering known as a constitutional convention, though this method has never been employed).

A **flexible constitution** is one that requires no special procedure for amendment. For example, provisions of the British Constitution are not entrenched. Law of the constitution can be modified, or indeed replaced, in the same way as any other law.

However, the formal process of amendment is not necessarily the best guide to the rigidity or flexibility of a constitution. For example, the US Constitution has been changed through judicial interpretation by the Supreme Court. On the other hand, some parts of the British Constitution, such as the hereditary basis of the Monarchy, have remained unchanged.

THE UNITARY BRITISH CONSTITUTION

FEDERAL AND UNITARY CONSTITUTIONS

In a **federal constitution**, as for example in the USA, Australia, Canada and Germany, sovereignty is divided between two levels of government. The federal government is sovereign in some matters and the governments of the constituent states or provinces are sovereign in others. Each within its own sphere exercises its power without control from the other. It is this feature which distinguishes a federal from a unitary constitution.

In a **unitary constitution** all sovereignty rests with the central government; if constituent provinces exist, they are subordinate authorities, deriving their power from the central legislature, which may overrule them at any time by the ordinary legal processes.

The Constitution of the United Kingdom of Great Britain and Northern Ireland is, like the constitutions of France or Sweden, unitary rather than federal. Parliament at Westminster is the supreme law making authority for the whole of the United Kingdom.

However, Britain might better be described as a union state rather than as a unitary state.

Unitary and union states

A unitary state is built up around one unambiguous political centre which enjoys economic dominance and pursues a more or less undeviating policy of administrative standardisation. All areas of the state are treated alike, and all institutions are directly under the control of the centre.

A union state is not the result of straightforward dynastic conquest. Incorporation of at least parts of its territory has occurred through personal dynastic union, for example by treaty, marriage or inheritance. Integration is less than perfect here. While administrative standardisation prevails over most of its territory, the consequences of personal union entail survival in some areas of pre-union rights and institutional infrastructure which preserve some degree of regional autonomy and serve as agencies of indigenous elite recruitment (Rokkan and Urwin).

The Act of Union of 1707 created a union of England and Scotland. Integration was less than perfect. Some pre-union rights and institutions were preserved, for example the Scottish legal system and the Church of Scotland.

The definition of devolution

Devolution is the delegation of central government powers without the giving up of sovereignty. For example, in Northern Ireland, where, by the Government of Ireland Act 1920, a separate Parliament was set up to legislate for the province in domestic matters, ultimate authority continued to rest with the United Kingdom Parliament. This latter body created and conferred powers on the Northern Ireland Parliament and was able at any time to change those powers, withdrawing them completely in 1972, or to make laws over-riding the laws made in Northern Ireland. In other words, what had been given by Westminster in 1920 was taken away by Westminster in 1972 with direct rule now introduced under the Northern Ireland (Temporary Provisions) Act.

The Government White Paper on Scottish Devolution (July 1997) stressed: 'The UK Parliament is and will remain sovereign.' However, in practice, devolution to Scotland will effectively limit the power of the UK Parliament to legislate for Scotland. The experience of devolution in Northern Ireland between 1921 and 1969 showed how difficult it was for the British Parliament actually to exert its theoretical supremacy. For example, the Government of Ireland Act 1920, which bestowed devolution upon Northern Ireland, laid down proportional representation in both local and parliamentary elections as a guarantee for minorities. In 1922 the Northern Ireland government proposed to abolish proportional representation in local elections, something it was entitled to do under the 1920 Act. The British government sought to veto the measure, but when the Northern Ireland government threatened to resign, the veto was withdrawn and the measure became law.

The only political circumstances in which the British Parliament will be able to exercise its supremacy in Scotland will be what Bogdanor calls 'pathological' ones of the kind that occurred in Northern Ireland after the troubles erupted in 1969.

In federal systems, on the other hand, despite guarantees of state and provincial rights, the powers of central government have expanded. For example, in the USA there have been forces reducing the powers of the states over the years (see below).

The case for federalism

1 *Gives regional and local interests a constitutionally guaranteed political voice.* The states or provinces exercise a range of autonomous powers and enjoy some measure of representation in central government, usually through the second chamber of the federal legislature. The second chamber represents the interests of the states, whereas the first chamber represents the interests of the state.
2 *The fragmentation of government creates a network of checks and balances that help to protect individual liberty.* Federal systems have usually been more effective in constraining politicians at the centre than have unitary systems.
3 *It provides an institutional mechanism through which fractured societies have maintained unity and coherence.* Federalism may be absolutely vital in order for ethnically diverse and regionally divided societies to co-exist. For example, the genius of federalism in the USA was perhaps less that it provided the basis for unity amongst the 13 original states and more that it invested the USA with an institutional mechanism which enabled it to absorb the strains that immigration exerted from the mid-nineteenth century onwards.

The case against federalism

1 *There is a tendency towards centralisation.* The powers of central government have expanded in federal systems, largely as a result of the growth of economic and social intervention, together with central government's own greater revenue-raising capacities.
   For example, the US Constitution initially operated according to the principles of Dual Federalism, which emphasised central and state governments exercising sovereignty in their own spheres of activity. This view was based on the Tenth Amendment to the Constitution which reserved to the states all powers not specifically delegated to the federal government in the Constitution. However, formal constitutional devices do not in themselves determine what happens politically. After 1933, Co-operative Federalism emerged when states were required to act in a partnership with the national government and implement programmes to alleviate the effects of the Depression for which they received financial aid. The main mechanism to secure such co-ordinated action was the 'grant in aid' provided by the federal government.

The main features of the 'New Federalism', that is powers back to the state and fewer tied grants, were related to the polices of its proponents Nixon and Reagan (Republican Presidents of the USA for the periods 1969-74 and 1981-9), that is a concern for reducing budget deficit.

2 *Structures intended to create healthy tension within a system of government may also generate frustration and paralysis.* One of the weaknesses of federal systems is that, by constraining central authority, they make the implementation of bold economic or social programmes more difficult. For example, in the USA F.D. Roosevelt's New Deal was significantly weakened by Supreme Court decisions that were intended to prevent federal government from encroaching on the responsibilities of states. The progress of civil rights has been impeded by the ability of Southern state governments to resist or slow down the implementation of such legislation.

3 *It may strengthen centrifugal pressures and ultimately lead to disintegration.* It has been argued that federal systems are inherently unstable, tending towards either the guaranteed unity which only a unitary system can offer or greater decentralisation and ultimate collapse. For example, federalism in Canada can be deemed a failure if its purpose was to construct a political union within which both French-speaking and English-speaking populations can live in harmony.

THE ESSENTIAL PRINCIPLES OF THE BRITISH CONSTITUTION

The nineteenth century constitutional lawyer, A.V. Dicey, asserted in 1885 that the two principles which pervade the whole of what he called the English constitution were the sovereignty of parliament and the Rule of Law.

PARLIAMENTARY SOVEREIGNTY

The principle of parliamentary sovereignty, he declared, means that Parliament has 'the right to make or unmake any law whatever; and, further, that no person or body is recognised by the law of England as having a right to override or set aside the legislation of Parliament (Dicey). Its superior position to common law is ironic, given that the principle itself is a judicially self-imposed rule derived from common law. Hood Phillips, a twentieth century constitutional lawyer, has called it 'the one fundamental law of the British Constitution'.

THE RULE OF LAW

According to Dicey, the Rule of Law had three meanings:

1 *the absence of arbitrary power on the part of the government:* 'It means, in the first place, the absolute supremacy or predominance of regular law as opposed to

the influence of arbitrary power, and excludes the existence of arbitrariness, of prerogative, or even of wide discretionary authority on the part of the government.'

2 *that every man is subject to ordinary law administered by ordinary tribunals:* 'It means, again, equality before the law, or the equal subjection of all classes to the ordinary law of the land administered by the ordinary law courts.'
3 *that general rules of constitutional law are the result of the ordinary law of the land:* 'We may say that the constitution is pervaded by the rule of law on the ground that the principles of the constitution (as for example the right to personal liberty, or the right of public meeting) are with us the result of judicial decisions determining the rights of private persons brought before the courts.'

Definitions of the Rule of Law vary. Its primary meaning is that everything must be done according to law. But the Rule of Law demands something more since otherwise it would be satisfied by giving the government unrestricted discretionary powers, so that everything it did would then be within the law. The secondary meaning of the Rule of Law, therefore, according to H.W.R Wade, is that 'government should be conducted within a framework of recognised rules and principles which restrict discretionary power'.

Dicey himself recognised that parliamentary sovereignty and the Rule of Law might appear to stand in opposition to each other. He reconciled the two principles by stressing the internal checks and balances within the political system.

THE EUROPEAN UNION DIMENSION

Membership of the European Community, now the European Union, has injected a new judicial dimension into the constitution of each member state. The impact of this new judicial dimension has been particularly profound in Britain.

Under the terms of membership of the European Union, if there is a conflict between the provisions of European law and United Kingdom law, then the European law is to prevail. The 1972 European Communities Act stated that any dispute over the interpretation of Community treaties, and the laws made under them, was to be treated as a matter of law. Under the provisions of the Treaty of Rome, cases which reach the highest domestic court of appeal, in the case of Britain the House of Lords, must be referred to the European Court of Justice (ECJ), sitting in Luxembourg, for a final ruling.

Lower courts may also request a ruling from the ECJ on the meaning and interpretation of the treaties. There is no appeal against a decision of the ECJ and the powers of the court have been further extended by the Maastricht Treaty (1993). That confers on the court the power to fine member states for failing to comply with its judgements.

The effect of membership of the EU has therefore been to give a new role to the British courts and to introduce a new dimension in the form of the ECJ. Where the courts have ruled that British law conflicts with European Union law, then the British government has introduced legislation to bring British law into line with European Union law. From the moment of British membership, the courts have thus enjoyed a new and powerful position. That position was enhanced dramatically as a result of the ruling in the Factortame case.

The Factortame case

In 1993 the then European Economic Community introduced national fishing quotas in order to prevent overfishing in European waters.

Britain decided to put a stop to the practice known as 'quota hopping' whereby fishing quotas were 'plundered' by vessels flying the British flag but lacking any genuine link with Britain. Under the Merchant Shipping Act 1988, vessels registered as British had to satisfy conditions of nationality, residence and domicile.

Factortame Ltd. and other companies owned 95 fishing vessels which failed to satisfy one or more of the conditions because they were managed or controlled from Spain or by Spanish nationals. They challenged the legality of the 1988 Act on the grounds that it contravened European law.

The case reached the highest British court of appeal, the House of Lords, which ruled in 1990 that if the validity of an English statute is to be challenged in the European Court, the balance of convenience may require the English courts to prevent the government from enforcing the statute pending the European Court's decision, even if that is contrary to the interests of British citizens.

In 1991 the European Court of Justice ruled that the conditions laid down by legislation for the registration of fishing vessels must comply with the Community law. Provisions in the Merchant Shipping Act 1988 which require nationality, residence and domicile conditions to be satisfied before a fishing vessel can be registered as British were discriminatory and contrary to article 52 of the EEC Treaty.

The ruling in the Factortame case struck at the principle of parliamentary sovereignty. The ECJ was saying that British courts did have the power to set aside Acts passed by Parliament. This power was implicit in the terms of membership accepted by Britain, but it was now being made explicit.

Parliament retains the power to repeal the 1972 European Communities Act and thus effectively remove Britain from membership of the European Union. Furthermore, if Parliament passed an Act explicitly over-riding a provision of European law, it is presumed that the British courts would enforce the Act passed by Parliament. However, the chances of the 1972 Act being repealed are slim. It is also highly unlikely that Parliament will explicitly over-ride any European law.

THE EFFECT OF BRITISH MEMBERSHIP

It would seem reasonable to conclude that the effect of British membership of the European Union has been profound.

- One of the essential elements of the traditional constitution, the principle of parliamentary sovereignty, is challenged by the new dimensions created by membership.
- The principle of the Rule of Law is not affected, but there is now a new layer of judicial enforcement independent of the nation state. Citizens of the European Union are given rights under the European treaties, and the final interpretation of those treaties lies not with the British courts but with the European Court of Justice.
- The unitary nature of the state is under pressure, the regional emphasis adopted by the European Union having placed greater emphasis on sub-national government. Funds often flow from the European Union direct to regional bodies, and there is pressure for greater devolution of powers in England to elected regional assemblies.

REFORM OF THE BRITISH CONSTITUTION

THE CASE FOR A WRITTEN OR CODIFIED CONSTITUTION

1. *It is necessary in order to limit government.* Lord Hailsham (Lord Chancellor, 1970-74) called his Richard Dimbleby Lecture in 1976 'Elective dictatorship'. There had been, he said, an enlargement in the scale and range of government. At the same time, there had been a change in the relative influence of the different elements in government, so as to place all the effective powers in the hands of one of them; in other words, the checks and balances had largely disappeared.
   Power had centralised itself more and more in the House of Commons, more on the government side of the House, and more on the front benches. The House of Lords was not an effective balancing factor. Its influence on government was far weaker than that of second chambers in other countries, like the senate in the USA. The centre of gravity in the House of Commons had moved decisively towards the government side, the opposition gradually being reduced to impotence. When backbenchers showed promise, they were soon absorbed into the government and so lost their powers of independent action. The actual members of the government, with their parliamentary private secretaries, were one of the largest and most disciplined single groups in the House. None of them, so long as they retained their positions, could exercise an independent judgement.

The time allotted for debate of individual measures had become progressively less and less. Now it was the whips and the party caucus (organisation of the party in the House) which dominated the parliamentary scene. The increasing complexity of government made meticulous research and specialisation almost indispensable for speaking in Parliament. Ministers had disproportionate influence in debate as a result of their possession of the Civil Service brief.

So the sovereignty of Parliament has increasingly become, in practice, the sovereignty of the Commons, and the sovereignty of the Commons has increasingly become the sovereignty of the government, which, in addition to its influence in Parliament, controls the party whips, the party machine, and the civil service. This means that what has always been an elective dictatorship in theory, but one in which the component parts operated, in practice, to control one another, has become a machine in which one of those parts has come to exercise a predominant influence over the rest.

The Listener, *21 October 1976*

2 *It is inevitable.* Britain has committed itself to a number of international obligations, most notably membership of the European Union. Under the terms of membership, European Union law takes precedence over British law. The principle of parliamentary sovereignty remains formally intact in the sense that Parliament retains the power to repeal the 1972 European Communities Act, but so long as it remains on the statute book, the greater is the eroding impact of European Union membership on the principle.
Growing pressure for greater independence from government decision-making in London led to the decision of the incoming Labour government in 1997 to introduce elected assemblies in Scotland and Wales, with legislative and executive powers being given to those assemblies.

THE CASE AGAINST A WRITTEN OR CODIFIED CONSTITUTION

1 *It is unnecessary.* It is argued that the existing part-written but uncodified Constitution serves the country reasonably well and does not have the defects that critics ascribe to it. The existing system, it is argued, retains the checks and balances that Dicey identified in the nineteenth century. Government may usually get its way, but it does not always do so. It is limited by virtue of the fact that Parliament, in the period since 1970, has become more independent in its behaviour. The government can no longer take Parliament for granted in the same way that it could prior to 1970. It has been more prone to the threat and the actuality of parliamentary defeat since 1970 than at any other time in the twentieth century. The problem of Conservative governments in the 1990s was one of the government weakness, not strength.

2 *It is undesirable.* It would involve a shift of power from an elected body, Parliament, which is accountable to the electorate, to an unelected body, the judiciary, which is not. Judges may interpret the Constitution in a way that does not accord with the prevailing climate of opinion within the community.

> *Why it should be supposed that elderly lawyers with cautious and backward looking habits of thought are qualified to overrule the judgements of democratically elected legislators as to what is, in the circumstances of the time, justified, I do not profess to understand.*
>
> *Lord McClusky (former High Court judge and Solicitor General for Scotland), 1986 Reith Lectures, BBC*

PROBLEMS THAT WOULD ARISE IF BRITAIN WERE TO ADOPT A WRITTEN OR CODIFIED CONSTITUTION

How the legitimacy of a written constitution could be assured

In popular usage, legitimacy denotes the acceptance or recognition of what is appropriate. Applied to constitutional matters, legitimacy may be regarded as attaching to the document, the 'Constitution', that establishes the framework of the constitution. In this case, legitimacy will probably attach to the framework itself as well, as long as it conforms to the requirements of the constitution and does not become overlaid or undermined with inconsistent systems of power, as happened with the power of the Communist Party in the former USSR (the constitutions of 1936 and 1977 were subverted by the party).

But legitimacy should also attach to what government or the state does, to how it reaches decisions and to who makes and implements decisions: these matters will not necessarily be provided for in the constitution and, even if they are, the outcome may not be legitimate.

Although legitimating procedures may ensure that a constitution has the support of the majority of the people at the time, it does not of course follow that the content of the constitution is legitimate. The people could well vote in a **referendum** for, or a democratically elected Parliament could well adopt, a constitution that turned out to be neither democratic nor effective. The issues are bound to be complex, there may well be a background of horse-dealing between politicians before the terms of a constitution are agreed, and the people may be doing more than, or other things than, endorsing or refusing to endorse when voting. For example, they may be influenced by a desire to express approval or disapproval for the government of the day. Nor does a legitimating process mean that a majority of the people will continue to regard the constitution as legitimate for the foreseeable future. For example, a document that discriminates against minorities may have the support of the majority when it is adopted, but it may come to be regarded as illegitimate in due course because of its discriminatory provisions.

Legitimacy in the sense of public acceptance requires more than popular approval some years ago. Although a degree of legitimacy attaches to the way in which a written constitution was introduced – and this aspect of legitimacy may of course continue to be regarded as satisfactory, and in that sense legitimate indefinitely – it may not always be satisfactory: approval of a constitution by a majority of male voters in an imaginary nineteenth century state would not be regarded by the electorate in a twentieth-century state as having legitimated the measure for good.

As well as the procedure by which it came to be adopted, legitimacy has also to attach to the substance of a constitution, and ideas about this sort of legitimacy may change. A constitution that entrenched the power of one party – as with the constitutions of the former USSR and some other Eastern European countries, which entrenched the 'leading role' of the Communist parties - may come to seem illegitimate, regardless of how that provision crept into the constitution.

How much of a constitution ought to be justiciable

The principal provisions of the constitutions of the USA, Germany and France, for example, are 'justiciable' in the sense that issues about the constitutionality of acts of state bodies can be taken to the courts, or to a special Supreme or Constitutional Court, and adjudicated upon.

However, not all provisions of such constitutions are justiciable in this way. For example, under the Constitution of the French Fifth Republic, legislation before the Parliament can be subjected to scrutiny by the Constitutional Council which may report to the Parliament if in its view proposed legislation is 'unconstitutional'; but if the Parliament insists on passing the law despite such a report, there is no jurisdiction in the courts or any other body to hold it invalid. Other examples of 'non-justiciable' laws or actions include what in the USA are known as 'political questions' – the doctrine that courts have no authority to interfere with the discretionary authority of the other agencies of government. A question becomes political by a judge's refusal to decide it.

The inclusion of non-justiciable provisions, especially non-justiciable 'rights', in a constitution raises serious issues about the status of a constitution and the attitude of the public to it. Experience in the former USSR with the 1936 and 1937 constitutions, many provisions of which were not justiciable, contributed to the cynicism of the public about the system of government generally. If provisions are not legally enforceable, then the public is left at the mercy of politicians for the protection of its rights, and even a democratically elected parliamentary cannot be counted on to protect the rights of citizens.

Whereas civil and political rights are in principle justiciable, economic and social rights do not readily lend themselves to enforceability in the courts. Although in principle government ought to make provision for economic and social rights, this can only be done by detailed legislation.

How much detail a written constitution should contain

The amount of detail that goes into a constitution depends in part on the complexity of the system of government and in part on the purposes for which a constitution is being adopted. Hence the Constitution of India is 250 pages long, while the Constitutions of the USA and the Fifth French Republic are much shorter.

The relationship between a constitution and the previous system of government clearly affects the amount of detail that has to go into the constitution. However, there are further considerations that affect the amount of detail that is put into a constitution. If it is a purpose of a written constitution to map out the system of government coherently in one document so that it can be readily accessible to those who wish to find out about the system, then it makes sense to be fairly fully set out in that one document. Or if the desire is to overhaul the system in a wide range of respects, then this again argues for a detailed single document. On the other hand, if the main object of the constitution-making exercise is limited to giving additional protection to civil and political rights and to entrenching certain basic provisions, then relatively little detail is required.

The setting out of constitutional values and the establishment of new institutions and procedures are further reasons for a high level of detail in a constitution, but in the process the constitution becomes less accessible to the lay reader than a shorter document.

What the hierarchy of laws should be – whether some laws should be entrenched, and if so how

It would be perfectly possible for a constitution to provide different ways of amending its provisions according to the importance of the provision. Some of its provisions could be amendable by two-thirds of all members of both Houses of Parliament, and others by a referendum. Another method of entrenchment that could be employed is a requirement that the second chamber consent to amending legislation.

Whether a constitution can be, or should be, politically neutral

If we operate on the assumption that no person or organisation is infallible and that the people need to be protected against the fallibility of their governors and bad government, as well as against their own fallibility, what is needed is a finely balanced system of checks and balances to provide the necessary protection. However, within this set of checks and balances, the legislature could pass any law, and there would therefore be scope for a wide range of political parties to win power and for policy to be influenced by a range of ideologies from capitalism to socialism, always assuming that ideologies are fallible. In other words, it should be possible to create a 'neutral' constitution, but only operating within this set of principles.

However, some would criticise this sort of neutrality for envisaging only a minimum role for the state. In other words, it may be said not to be neutral as between competing ideologies.

SUMMARY

The British Constitution is part-written but uncodified.

It is a unitary constitution. The essential principles of the British Constitution are the sovereignty of parliament and the Rule of Law.

The impact of membership of the European Union has been to challenge the essential elements of the constitution.

A written or codified constitution is seen as necessary in order to limit government, and as inevitable given Britain's international obligations and pressure for greater devolution of powers in England. It is seen as unnecessary because government is limited, and as undesirable because it would, in effect, transfer power from an elected body, Parliament, to an unelected body, the judiciary.

The issues raised by written constitutions are legitimacy, justiciability, detail in a constitution, the hierarchy of laws in a constitution, and whether a constitution can be neutral.

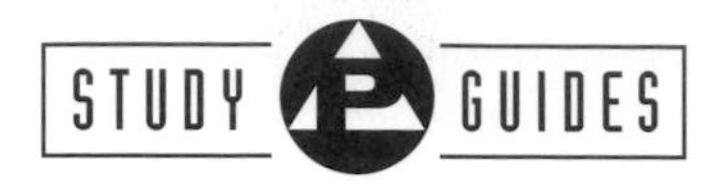

Revision Hints

Make sure you understand the term constitution, and can distinguish between written and unwritten, rigid and flexible, federal and unitary constitutions. You should be able to explain why it is sometimes difficult in practice to distinguish clearly between the different types of constitution.

Know the 'essential principles' of the British Constitution and understand its European Union dimension.

You should be able to argue for and against federalism, as well as whether Britain should have a written constitution, and to consider the broad issues raised by written constitutions.

Exam Hints

Answering short questions on 'The British Constitution in Context'

1 a Distinguish between a federal and a unitary constitution.
b Outline a case for and against a federal Britain.

You should be able to distinguish in general terms between the two types of constitution. Where comparative examples are quoted, the knowledge indicated should not be superficial. Do not drift into the issue of federalism within a European context or mention very generally the issue of local government versus central government.

Answering essay questions on 'The British Constitution in Context'

1 'The impact of membership of the European Union has been to challenge the essential elements of the British Constitution.' Discuss.

Do not ignore the constitutional point of the question; also, do not refer to the arguments for and against membership of the EU, or to the views of the political parties. Do not confuse the European Convention on Human Rights with the European Court of Justice. 'Loss of sovereignty' is the common theme, and use your knowledge of the consequences of the 1972 European Communities Act. Explain also the Factorame case.

Practice Questions

1 a Distinguish between a rigid and a flexible construction.
b Why is it sometimes difficult to distinguish clearly between the two?
2 State a case for and a case against a written constitution for the United Kingdom.

3

THE BRITISH SYSTEM OF PARLIAMENTARY GOVERNMENT IN CONTEXT

Introduction

THIS CHAPTER WILL define the doctrine of the separation of powers. It will distinguish between parliamentary and presidential systems of government.

The question of whether the British system is becoming presidential will then be addressed. Finally, the relationship between the executive and the legislature in the British system of government will be analysed.

Key Points

- A definition of the separation of powers.
- The distinction between parliamentary and presidential systems of government.
- The rise of a British presidency?
- The relationship between the executive and legislature in the British system of government.

SEPARATION OF POWERS

A pure doctrine of the **separation of powers** might be defined as follows:

- Separation of agencies: it is essential for the establishment and maintenance of political liberty that the government be divided into three branches or agencies: the **legislature**, the **executive** and the **judiciary**. In Britain these branches are referred to as Parliament, government and the courts.

- Separation of functions: for each of these three branches, there is a corresponding identifiable function of government: legislative, or law-making; executive, or law-application; and judicial or law-adjudication.
- Each branch of government must be confined to the exercise of its own function and not be allowed to intrude upon the functions of the other branches.
- Separation of persons: the persons who compose these three agencies of government must be kept separate and distinct, with no individual allowed to be at the same time a member of more than one branch.
- In this way, each of the branches will be a check to the others, and no single group of people will be able to control the machinery of the state.

The doctrine has rarely been held in this pure form, and even more rarely been put into practice, but all these elements must be true to some extent for it to be a concept used to describe a system of government.

THE USA

The USA's hatred of the corruption in and excessive influence of the British legislature, on which the Americans blamed much of the conflict between Parliament and the colonies, led the USA to accept a separation of persons into legislative and executive branches.

BRITAIN

By contrast, Walter Bagehot in 1867 described the 'efficient' secret of what he called the English Constitution, 'that by which it, in fact, works and rules', as 'the close union, the nearly complete fusion, of the executive and legislative powers' (in *The English Constitution*, listed at the end of the book).

PARLIAMENTARY AND PRESIDENTIAL SYSTEMS OF GOVERNMENT

HEADS OF STATE

The head of state in a parliamentary system of government may be a monarch, as in Britain, Japan and Sweden, or a president, as in Germany, India and Italy. He or she is a nominal head of state whose functions are chiefly formal and ceremonial and whose political influence is limited. For example, in Britain, the Queen 'reigns but does not rule': most of her political functions are in practice exercised by Her (elected) Ministers.

The head of state in a presidential system of government is both the nominal and the political head of state. For example, the President of the USA has some political power.

THE SELECTION OF THE POLITICAL EXECUTIVE

In a parliamentary system of government, the chief executive (the Prime Minister of Britain or the Chancellor of Germany) together with the Cabinet form part of the legislature, and are selected by the legislature. For example, in Britain the Prime Minister is a Member of Parliament, selected by the House of Commons, and the Cabinet comprises either MPs or members of the House of Lords.

In a presidential system of government the political executive is not part of the legislature or selected by the legislature, but the president is directly elected by the electorate. For example, in the USA the President and his Cabinet cannot be members of Congress – that is either the House of Representatives or the Senate – and the President is elected directly by the electorate.

THE REMOVAL OF THE POLITICAL EXECUTIVE

In a parliamentary system of government, the political executive can be removed by the legislature if the legislature withdraws its support. For example, in Britain the Callaghan government requested a dissolution of Parliament when defeated on a specific issue of confidence in 1979 and, on losing the subsequent General Election, resigned.

In a presidential system of government the president cannot be removed from office by the legislature except through the legal process of **impeachment**.

THE RISE OF A BRITISH PRESIDENCY?

Michael Foley asserts that by employing perspectives drawn from the American presidency, it is possible to show that the prime ministerial leadership has undergone changes since the late 1970s so profound that they amount to a qualitative shift in the type of leadership that is now viable in the British system of government. These changes were due partly to the effect of Margaret Thatcher's long tenure of office, but they have deeper roots than this. The significance of Thatcher's premiership lies more in the way that it brought to the surface new and fundamental sources of leadership that had previously been associated with the American presidency, but which have since been shown not to be limited to that office.

SPATIAL LEADERSHIP

British prime ministers have begun to experience and to exploit the opportunities for demonstrating leadership by the creation of a sense of distance, and occasionally detachment, from government.

- Beginning with *Margaret Thatcher* (Prime Minister, 1979–90), prime ministers have increasingly made highly publicised intercessions into the Whitehall machinery. These are made not in the style of a managing director seeking to protect and strengthen the organisation, but more to enhance the political position of the prime minister at the expense of the organisational integrity of the government.
- *John Major* (Prime Minister, 1990–97) came to embody and even to dramatise his own 'big idea' of the Citizen's Charter, its aim being to return power to the consumer by establishing performance standards and more effective complaints procedures and giving various rights of redress when public services broke their obligations.
- *Tony Blair's* senior staff made it clear in May 1997 that the Prime Minister's Office was to control Whitehall departments in a much more direct and personal way than ever before. Press Secretary Alistair Campbell had informed all departmental press chiefs that media bids for interviews with their ministers must be cleared first with him. This followed the appointment of Peter Mandelson as Minister without Portfolio to keep a close eye on other ministers on Blair's behalf. The Prime Minister had also appointed Sally Morgan as his Political Secretary, and it was to be her job to make sure that the party 'marches in step' with the government.

PRESIDENTIAL BLAIR?

THE EDINBURGH CONFERENCE CENTRE, DURING THE COMMONWEALTH HEADS OF GOVERNMENT MEETING, OCTOBER 1997

THE CULT OF THE 'OUTSIDER'

Linked to spatial leadership is the increasingly common strategy of prime ministers claiming that they are outsiders.

- *Margaret Thatcher* considered herself, and was widely regarded by others, to be an outsider. This outlook was probably drawn first and foremost from her background as a grocer's daughter in Grantham during the Great Depression, and from the nonconformist background to her Methodist upbringing. Her leadership was based upon the notion that government itself was the overriding issue in contemporary politics. This outlook was partly rooted in her self-image as an outsider, excluded from the party's establishment and standing apart from the prevailing political ideas and practices. It was also based upon the circumstances of her political position – her policy was not shared by a majority of the Conservative Party or even by a majority of her own Cabinet.
- *John Major* had direct experience of hard times. When his father's business manufacturing garden gnomes collapsed, the family had to move to a top-floor two-room flat in Coldharbour Lane, Brixton, which had a gas ring on the landing and a shared toilet on the ground floor. Major felt obliged to leave school early to help the family finances. He was unemployed for a time in his youth. From this humble background he had risen through a career at the Standard Chartered Bank and through local politics in Lambeth Council to be prime minister. He held high office, but in every other respect he appeared to remain an outsider, linked to that wider public which could identify with him and his principles.
- *Tony Blair* came from a more privileged background, educated at Fetters College, an Edinburgh public school, and Oxford University. However, he also sought to exploit his appeal as an outsider. 'I think I stand outside politics sometimes', he told Lesley White in an interview for the *Sunday Times Magazine*, 20 April 1997. He yearned to be free from the Labour Party's bond with the trade unions in order to appeal to the great mass outside the party. In making his first speech to the Trades Union Congress as prime minister in September 1997, an abrasive Blair warned the trade unions to modernise or die, telling them 'it's warmer in the real world'.

PUBLIC LEADERSHIP

Public contact, or at least the 'common touch', used to be an important consideration in a prospective prime minister. With the emergence of a much less hierarchical social order, a leader's relationship with the public is now central and decisive. He or she must have the ability to appeal to the public's own criteria for leadership in an increasingly volatile society. As political parties are no longer reliable vehicles of public mobilisation in the more fluid conditions of independent voters, they condone, and even exploit, 'leadership stretch' – the acquisition by the leader of as much discretion as possible. Each does so in order to increase its chances of translating the leader's role as party spokesperson into the party's point of access into government.

Leaders need to maintain their access to the public and, therefore, their dominance of the media, in order to retain the confidence of their parties and the credibility of their claims to national leadership. Potential and actual prime ministers can no longer afford to be displaced by other leaders, or by other members of their own party, in what has become a continual process of public engagement. Instead, they are propelled to acquire as much freedom of action as possible in order to optimise their party's political objectives.

THE PERSONAL FACTOR

Increasingly, party leaders are expected not merely to provide a tangible representation of their party's collective nature, but also to offer a singular and integrated image of the party and its programmes. Even recently, a party leader could be seen primarily as a salesman's boot in the public's door, gaining attention for the company's wares and seeking to put them in the best possible light. Today, a leader is not merely the boot. He or she constitutes the suitcase as well. It is he or she who must satisfy the public's aroused interest in the political agenda of executive leadership, impress his or her leadership credentials directly upon the populace, and raise public confidence in his or her party by virtue of its capacity to provide leadership. Even voting-behaviour specialists, who used to dismiss the influence of leaders upon popular support, are taking the linkage more seriously than used to be the case.

As party leaders have risen to, and been propelled into, positions of greater prominence, differences between the parties have become increasingly personalised in nature. This has led to a growing distinction between the level of popular support given to leaders and the degree of approval given to the policies of their parties. Personal considerations and leadership appraisal influence the public's estimation of a party's fitness for government. The volume of opinion polls on leadership, together with the prominence given to the poll results, reflect the rise of publicly perceived and assessed 'leadership attributes' as separate and substantive categories of political evaluation. The public is regularly asked to assess and to rate the personal qualities of the prime minister and his or her competitors in the assumption that the public's appraisal of selected components of personality are central to the estimation, and ultimately the reality, of contemporary political leadership. See the chart on p 25.

Percentage of the population associating these descriptions with each party leader	Tony Blair: Tony Blair 97	Tony Blair: Tony Blair 96	William Hague	Paddy Ashdown
TOUGH	57	45	15	37
ARROGANT	21	39	44	21
UNDERSTANDS PEOPLE LIKE ME	65	50	11	38
HAS LOTS OF PERSONALITY	80	54	8	35
MORE HONEST THAN MOST POLITICIANS	54	32	9	37
EXPERIENCED	33		8	64
HAS MORE SYTLE THAN SUBSTANCE	50		21	20

AN ICM POLL ON THE PARTY LEADER'S PERSONAL QUALITIES.
SOURCE: *THE GUARDIAN*, 8 OCTOBER 1997.

A leader is now expected to possess an individual sense of vision for the party and the country. The authority of such a vision is often publicly declared to be integral to the leader's personal background and experience. Just as the personal origins can support a leader's claim to the right to propound a public vision, so the formative influences and lifetime accomplishments contribute to the personal nature of their vision.

The state of the parties, their programmes, reputations and fitness for office, are increasingly refracted through the lens of leadership figures. Leadership has changed from being a position held by a person to one which is characterised by, and dependent upon, the idiosyncratic properties of the leaders. Today prime ministers speak more in the first person than they used to do. John Major, when asked to comment in the 1992 General Election result, summed up the Conservative Party victory: 'I'm delighted to have my own mandate. I think it is very important. I can now accept that the country has elected me in my own right to be Prime Minister' (quoted in *The Times*, 11 April 1992). He continued: 'I now have a clear majority … . I am prime minister of all this country, for everyone, whether they voted for me or not' (quoted in *The Guardian*, 14 April 1992).

The health and mental fitness of prime ministers are openly discussed. Their parentage and origins, their childhood and formative experiences, their diets, tastes and pastimes, together with their wives and children, are all regarded as suitable subjects for exposure and assessment because they all help to convey that leadership is a personal resource.

OTHER INFLUENCES

Another factor shaping the office of the prime minister is the ever more intense mass media concentration upon prime ministers, and especially the marked priority given to them over their immediate political colleagues. The mass media, especially the electronic media, give pronounced emphasis to the leaders as individual political figures, and to public leadership as an over-riding political issue. Just as prime ministers are increasingly dependent upon the mass media for the links to the world outside Whitehall and Westminster, so the mass media are increasingly reliant upon prime ministers for news coverage and for sources of political speculation. This interdependency is particularly evident during elections when the volume and priority of daily news coverage is geared conspicuously to the contenders for the office of prime minister.

A further factor is the onset of a presidential emphasis upon the state, and even the destiny, of the nation. Both can serve to support prime ministerial claims to represent the national interest and the general welfare. Integral to this development is the importance of foreign policy in increasing the exposure and identity of a prime minister as a national leader. In particular, the rising prominence of international summitry affords the prime minister the opportunity to publicly perform the quasi-presidential role of speaking for the nation. In doing so, the prime minister is regularly portrayed as set apart from party and Cabinet, and from what are made to seem to be merely the domestic pre-occupations of the other party leaders.

The prime minister's position and powers have also acted as a catalyst in the generation of the public's renewed consciousness of the content and value of constitutional principles. The symbolic and actual representation of central executive power in concentrated form has helped to introduce a political debate and a political language similar to that which American presidents have long been accustomed to working with – namely, a close interest in the origins, location, legitimacy and distribution of power; a concern over the principles of its usage; and a desire to ensure that power is limited by legally enforceable restraints and by the existence of entrenched rights and liberties. In essence, the very prominence of central executive power has become a litmus test to assess the effectiveness of the constitutional ideal of a 'government under law'.

THE OVERALL EFFECT

The net effect of all these influences is the emergence in Britain of a full-scale and sophisticated politics of leadership focusing both upon the relative merits and competitive behaviour of leaders, and on the meaning, usefulness, value, sources and location of leadership within the political system. The requirements and expectations of leadership have generated an entire medium of political exchange, in which a specialised vocabulary and set of evaluative categories has grown up through which leaders are observed and appraised. Leaders still remain utterly dependent upon political parties for their formal position and initial platform, as well as for their access to government. However, it is also true to say that the leaders of the parties in Britain increasingly occupy a world of their own.

This world might well be called 'leaderland'. It is dominated by the need for leaders to have leadership qualities, to have the opportunity to demonstrate these, and to have them publicly appreciated. Leadership is watched, tested and assessed for its public qualities by a public increasingly interested in the public performance of leaders. Leadership has now become an established political issue in its own right. The issue is played out in public, not least because it is this arena in which the issue is most significant. It is the arena in which the varying conceptions of leadership, and the differing estimations of leaders in fulfilling these conceptions, are discussed and debated. Not only are leaders constantly on show in such an arena, they have to be on permanent parade in order to remain leaders. It is no longer enough to be a political leader who merely appears in public. Leaders now have to possess the qualities to lead the public, or at least to make a plausible assertion to be able to lead the public. They have to do well not just as party leaders but also as public figures in the unrelenting exposure of leaderland, where they are judged not just by party criteria but also by more volatile public criteria generated by, and applied through, leaderland itself. As a result, the competition for the office of prime minister is increasingly a public contest about public leadership by public leaders.

The British prime minister has evolved, and is evolving, away from what a prime minister used to be. British premiership has to all intents and purposes turned, not into a British version of the American presidency, but into an authentically British presidency.

THE RELATIONSHIP BETWEEN THE EXECUTIVE AND THE LEGISLATURE

After 1867 the extension of the franchise from approximately one million votes to nearly two million resulted in the creation of the modern party system based upon a mass electorate. The necessity of maintaining a majority in the House of Commons by winning elections in the country at large resulted in strong party organisations which could mobilise party workers to get out the votes. The increased partisanship engendered by this system, and the need to maintain strict party discipline in the Commons, was the basis for the development of formidable party machines.

This swung the balance decisively in favour of the executive. For example, 1979 was the first occasion that a confidence vote in the House of Commons defeated a government since 1924.

SUMMARY

The British system of government is parliamentary with a nearly complete fusion of the executive and legislative powers, compared to a presidential system with a separation of powers.

British governments are selected by the legislature and can be removed by the legislature.

The British system of government has become increasingly presidential. Forces shaping the office of Prime Minister have been spatial leadership; cult of the 'outsider'; public leadership; the personal factor; and other influences.

After 1867, the extension of the franchise resulted in the creation of the modern party system based upon a mass electorate, which has swung the balance in favour of the executive.

Revision Hints

Make sure you understand the concept of the separation of powers and that you can distinguish between parliamentary and presidential systems of government.

You should be able to argue a case for the rise of a British presidency.

Make sure that you understand the relationship between the executive and the legislature in the British system of government.

4

BRITISH DEMOCRACY IN CONTEXT

Introduction

THIS CHAPTER WILL define democracy and then describe different types of democracy, including the distinctive features of **liberal democracy**. It will explain elitist, Marxist and radical criticisms of liberal democracy.

In looking at means through which people can participate directly in democracy, the distinction between a referendum and an initiative will be made, the case for and the case against referendums and initiatives will be considered, and the questions of when referendums should be held and how their use should be regulated will be examined.

Finally, the question of how accurate it is to describe the British system of government as liberal democratic will be examined, and the issue of how democratic accountability can be enhanced will be considered.

Key Points

- Definition and types of democracy.
- How can people participate directly in democracy?
- How liberally democratic is the British system of government?

THE DEFINITION OF DEMOCRACY

The classical conception of **democracy** is derived from the Ancient Greek words *demos*, meaning 'the many' or 'the people', and *kratos*, meaning 'power' or 'rule'. Democracy therefore means 'rule by the people' or 'the power of the people'.

Exam Hints

Answering short questions on 'The British System of Parliamentary Government in Context'

A typical example of a question on the British system of parliamentary government in context is:

1 a Distinguish between a parliamentary and a presidential system of government.

b How might the British political system be regarded as becoming presidential?

The first part of the question is straightforward. You would be expected to demonstrate a knowledge and understanding of parliamentary and presidential systems of government. The essence of a parliamentary system of government is that the executive branch of government is drawn from the legislature, to which it remains responsible. This can be contrasted with a presidential system of government marked by a separation of powers, in which members of the legislature are not permitted to be members of the executive. Good students would make this explicit in their answers. Weaker students would include much information about Parliament and the President in their answers and mention the legislative/executive link and non-link only in passing. While students would receive credit for such answers, they could not expect to score as highly as those who made the fundamental features of a parliamentary system and a presidential system clear from the very beginning of their answers.

In answer to part (b) of the question, you would be expected to demonstrate an ability to interpret and analyse political information, to apply a range of relevant political ideas, and to evaluate arguments. It could be argued that the British prime minister is in practice elected directly by the electorate. Most students would probably concentrate on the extent to which the executive is held to account by the legislature. Once the initial point is made in any answer, it is the depth and the detail which are important in determining the grade.

Practice Questions

1 a What do you understand by the 'separation of powers'?

b To what extent is there a separation of the executive and legislative powers in the British system of government?

2 'British premiership has to all intents and purposes turned, not into a British version of the American presidency, but into an authentically British presidency'. Discuss.

Abraham Lincoln, in his Gettysburg Address delivered in 1864 at the height of the American Civil War, extolled the virtues of what he called 'government of the people, by the people, and for the people'. Apart from making clear that democracy links government to the people, his definitition provides the principal distinction between two types of democracy:

1 **direct democracy** – government by the people
2 **indirect or representative democracy** – government for the people.

DIRECT DEMOCRACY

Direct democracy is the direct and continuous participation of citizens in the tasks of government. A form of direct democracy operated in Athens, the largest and most influential of the independent city-states into which Ancient Greece was divided. It was practicable, in this relatively small state, for the citizens to meet in one place for their deliberations, so that the process is often described as 'market place democracy'.

All major decisions were made by an assembly, to which all citizens belonged. This met regularly. When full-time public officials were needed, they were selected on the basis of lot (that is, by chance) or in rotation, and terms of office were typically short. A council consisting of 500 citizens acted as an executive or steering committee of the assembly, and a committee of 50 citizens, in turn, made proposals to the council. The president of the committee held office for only a single day, and no Athenian could hold this honour more than once in his lifetime. The only concession made to the need for training and experience was in the case of the 10 military generals who, unlike other public officials, were eligible for re-election.

However, Athenian democracy excluded the majority of the people from political participation. It was restricted to male citizens born in Athens who were over the age of 20, thereby excluding women, slaves and foreign residents.

LIBERAL DEMOCRACY

Liberal democracy is found in the so-called First World of industrialised Western countries, notably in North America and Western Europe. It has also spread into the 'Third World' of developing countries, such as the world's largest democracy, India, and the 'Second World' of former communist countries.

The distinctive features of liberal democracy are the liberal element of limited government (the idea that the individual should enjoy some protection from arbitrary government), and the democratic element of popular consent (the idea that government should in some way be tied to the will of the people).

LIMITED GOVERNMENT

The central concern of liberalism is to safeguard and enlarge individual freedom. From the liberal perspective, government is a necessary evil, always liable to become a tyranny against the individual if government power is not checked. This leads to support for effective limits to the exercise of government power. In practice, government can be limited in two ways, by outside or external constraints upon what government can do, and by internal constraints which seek to break up government power and prevent it being concentrated in the hands of a single person or body.

External constraints

- **Constitutionalism**, a system of government according to prescribed rules which imposes limits on the government. Written constitutions set significant limits to the exercise of government power when their provisions are **justiciable**.
- Protection of the rights of individuals. This can be entrenched in a **bill of rights** providing a legal definition of the rights of individuals in the relationships between them and the state. For example, the first 10 Amendments of the American Constitution are collectively called The Bills of Rights. (See Watts, *Protecting Rights in Brtiain*, 1998, Hodder & Stoughton; part of the Access to Politics series.)
- Belief in the Rule of Law, that is government conducted within a framework of recognised rules and principles which restrict discretionary power (power of the government to act at its discretion).
- The existence of **civil society**, comprising a range of autonomous groups, each enjoying some measure of independence from government.

Internal constraints

Government power is less in danger of becoming a tyranny if it is broken up or fragmented. The fragmentation of government into a number of power centres is designed to weaken government in two ways, by ensuring that each person or institution possesses only a portion of government power, and by creating internal rivalries amongst the institutions of government which serve to ensure that each can constrain the others. This leads to the checks and balances which are characteristic of a liberal system of government.

- The concept of the **separation of powers** (see Chapter 3).

- **Bicameralism**, that is the fragmentation of legislative power by the division of legislatures into two chambers. One chamber is able to check the power of the other, thereby limiting the power of government.
- The decentralisation of government power, achieved most radically by federalism (see Chapter 2).

DEMOCRATIC GOVERNMENT

- Liberal democracy is a form of indirect or representative democracy. Rule by the people means that the people participate not directly in government, but indirectly by electing representatives to govern them.
- There are regular elections conducted on the basis of **political equality**, founded on the idea of 'one person, one vote, one value'.
- Elections must be 'free' with the **electorate** able to develop its own political sympathies, expressing these freely and independently. This requires the existence of a secret ballot, designed to prevent intimidation or corruption at election time. It also requires a range of civil liberties such as freedom of expression, freedom of assembly and freedom of movement, sometimes referred to as **democratic rights**. (See '*Protecting Rights in Britain*' by Duncan Watts, also in the Access to Politics series.)
- Elections must be competitive, with the electorate presented with a choice of candidates and parties. The cornerstone of this type of democracy is **political pluralism,** that is the existence of a variety of political ideas and doctrines.

Liberal democracy is found only in states with a predominantly free-market, that is capitalist, economic system. With few, and mostly temporary, exceptions (such as South Africa), every capitalist state has had a liberal democratic political system.

Historically, the above-mentioned liberal element in liberal democracy emerged some time before the democratic element. Many 'First World' states became liberal years before they became democratic. For example, one person one vote was not brought into operation in Britain until 1948 when, by the Representation of the People Act, the university constituencies were abolished and the 'business premises qualification' was taken away.

ELITISM

Elitism is a belief that political power is concentrated in the hands of a few, namely the elite.

CLASSICAL ELITISM

Classical elitists believed elitism to be an inevitable, even desirable, feature of political life. For example:

- Mosca proclaimed that in all societies 'two classes of people appear – a class that rules and a class that is ruled'. In his view, the resources or attributes that are necessary for rule are always unequally distributed, and further, a cohesive minority will always be able to manipulate and control the masses.
- Pareto suggested that the qualities needed to rule are those of one or two psychological types, namely 'foxes' who rule by cunning and are able to manipulate the consent of the masses, and 'lions' whose domination is typically through coercion and violence.
- Michels stated that it is in the nature of all organisations, however democratic they might appear, for power to be concentrated in the hands of a small group of dominant figures who can organise and make decisions, rather than being in the hands of the apathetic rank and file. He called this 'the iron law of oligarchy'.

MODERN ELITISM

Modern elitists have tended to be more critical of elite rule. For example, C. Wright Mills argued that industrialised societies like the USA are dominated by a 'power elite', a small cohesive group that commands 'the major hierarchies and organisations of modern society'. In his view, power is largely vested in the non-elected bodies of the state system, including the military, the bureaucracy, the judiciary and the police. He argued, in fact, that the means for exercising power are more narrowly concentrated in a few hands in such societies than at any earlier time in history. From this perspective, the principle of political equality and the process of electoral competition upon which liberal democracy is founded are largely a sham.

DEMOCRATIC ELITISM

However, some modern elitists have argued that democracy is consistent with elite rule. For example, Schumpeter described the democratic method as 'that institutional arrangement for arriving at political decisions in which individuals acquire the power to decide by means of a competitive struggle for the people's vote'. The voter exercises the same power in the political market as the consumer does in economic markets.

This idea of 'democratic elitism' was developed by Downs. He believed that electoral competition creates, in effect, a political market, in which politicians act as entrepreneurs bent upon achieving government power, and individual voters behave like consumers, voting for the party whose policies most closely reflect their preferences. Downs argued that a system of open and competitive elections guarantees democratic rule because it places government in the hands of the party whose philosophy, values and policies correspond most closely to the preferences of the largest group of voters.

MARXISM

Marxists have criticised liberal democracy for being based on a narrow conception of political equality. They believe that political power reflects the unequal distribution of economic power and, in particular, the unequal ownership of wealth. Marxists argue that there is inherent tension between the political equality which liberal democracy proclaims and the social inequality which a capitalist economy inevitably generates. Liberal democracy is thus seen as 'capitalist' or 'bourgeois' democracy, manipulated and controlled by the entrenched power of a ruling class. Marxists believe that genuine democracy can only be brought about through the achievement of social equality, or what Marxists called **social democracy** (in its original sense).

PARTICIPATORY DEMOCRACY

Advocates of **participatory democracy** have returned to the classical conception of democracy and emphasised the need for participation by the people. The 'marketplace' democracy of Ancient Athens, however, is clearly impractical in modern nation-states. There are examples of township meetings in some New England communities of the USA and in the communal assemblies employed in the smaller Swiss cantons, but these are exceptions.

However, the town meeting is not the only means through which people can participate directly:

- a **referendum**, according to Butler and Ranney, is 'a vote of the people on a proposed law, policy or public expenditure'. In a number of states in the USA, statutory consultation (laid down by statute that there must be consultation by means of a referendum) is considered necessary on measures of constitutional change. Other states use legislative referendums, by which laws require a ratification vote – formal vote of approval – by the people. There are also popular referendums in which a group of citizens can hold a ballot (that is a vote) on some particular action of the legislature.
- an **initiative** is used in a large number of states in the USA.

REFERENDUMS AND INITIATIVES

Austin Ranney (in the US Information Agency) says that a referendum is an arrangement whereby a proposed law or policy that has been approved by a legislature does not go into force until it has been approved by the voters in an election (eg, the devolution referendum in Scotland, 1997.) An initiative, on the other hand, is an arrangement whereby any person or group of persons may draft a proposed law or constitutional amendment and, after satisfying certain requirements of numbers and form, have it referred directly to the voters for final approval or rejection (eg, Proposition 215 in California, 1996, on decriminalisation of the drug cannabis for treatment of diseases such as cancer and Aids). A referendum enables voters to accept or reject the legislature's proposals, while an initiative allows the voters both to make their own proposals and to vote upon the proposals of other voters.

Magleby (in Butler and Ranney) makes the distinction that a referendum permits voters to correct 'sins of commission' (laws or policy which legislature has committed itself to), while an initiative is a means to correct legislative 'sins of omission' (laws which legislature has omitted).

A **recall** is the power of the people to remove an elected offical before the end of his or her term of office.

The case for referendums and initiatives

- *They encourage participation and act as an education device.* As Dicey put it in 1894, they 'would bring men to the ballot-box who now hardly vote at all'.
- *They enable precision in posing and answering questions about what the voters want.* In contrast, the trouble with a general election is that the wishes of the voters may be unclear: some may vote for or against an issue, while others may wish to show support (or not) for the prime minister. As Dicey put it:

> *Under the referendum an elector may begin to find it possible to vote for or against a given law in accordance with his real view as to its merits or demerits, without being harassed through the knowledge that if he votes against a law which his conscience and his judgement condemns, he will also be voting that A, whom he deems the fittest man in England to be Prime Minister, shall cease to hold office, and that B, whom the elector happens to distrust, shall at once become Prime Minister*
>
> *A.V. Dicey,* Introduction to the Study of the Law of the Constitution, *8th edn, Macmillan, 1915.*

- *They offer constitutional protection, to prevent fundamental laws from being changed without the consent of the people.*
- *They act as instruments to remedy the defects of representative government.* 'It is certain', wrote Dicey in the introduction to the eighth edition of his *Law of the Constitution*, 'that no man who is really satisfied with the working of our party

system will ever look with favour on an institution which aims at correcting the vices of party government. By virtue of the overpowering legitimacy conferred by popular majorities, referendums usually break the political stalemates created by inflexible party systems. For example, proportional representation was adopted in New Zealand and modified in Italy after years of debate, and these changes are unlikely to be reversed for a generation.
Party government in Britain seems to work less effectively on Europe than on any other major issue. For example, at the 1992 General Election, all three main political parties were in favour of ratifying the Maastricht Treaty. Those who opposed European integration found themselves effectively unrepresented.

The case against referendums and initiatives

- *They undermine parliamentary sovereignty.*
- *Only elected politicians are in a position to judge complex issues.*
- *They undermine responsible government, understood here as a government pursuing a wise and consistent policy* (see Chapter 5). For example, the promoters of California's Proposition 13 in 1978 collected well over a million signatures to put forward the proposition that property taxes should be cut by 57 per cent and that the tax rate be cut from 3 per cent to 1 per cent of market value. This attracted the support of 65 per cent of the voters. However, what the voters had failed to realise was that such a measure would lead to drastic reductions in the provision of public services, notably the police and emergency services, and shortly afterwards the reduction had to be reversed.
- *They weaken representative government.* As John Mackintosh, Labour MP and academic, put it in a debate on the referendum on UK membership of the EC, in the House of Commons in 1975: 'The fundamental assumption behind the referendum is that this House does not adequately represent the feelings of the country.'

When should referendums be held?

1 *On issues involving the transfer of powers of Parliament.* While voters may be said to entrust their MPs with legislative power, they give them no authority to transfer that power. The idea that power is entrusted to the nation's representatives for specific purposes only has its origins in John Locke's philosophy who wrote in 1690 that the legislature 'cannot transfer the power of making laws to any other hands, for it being but a delegated power from the people, they who have it cannot pass it over to others'.

- Britain's first referendum was the poll on the border, 1973, in Northern Ireland on whether the powers of Parliament in Northern Ireland should be transferred to the Republic of Ireland. The referendum was held under the Northern Ireland Constitution Act, 1973, which provided for a border poll in Northern Ireland at intervals of not less than 10 years, and which also declared that there would be no change in Northern Ireland's constitutional status without the consent of the people of Northern Ireland as expressed in a referendum.

- Britains first nationwide referendum was in 1975 on whether there should be a major transfer of the powers of Parliament to the European Community. The question was whether Britain should remain in the European Community on the terms renegotiated by the Wilson Labour government.
- All three main political parties in 1997 were committed to a referendum on the single European currency.
- The devolution referendums of 1979 and 1997 in Scotland (see below) and Wales were concerned with whether powers of Parliament should be devolved to a Scottish Parliament (legislative devolution) and whether delegated powers of Parliament should be devolved to a Welsh Assembly (executive devolution).
- Tony Blair's Labour government announced in July 1997 that there would be a referendum in May 1998 on whether there should be a directly elected mayor in London and Greater London Authority.

HOW THEY VOTED

Voters were asked:

Q1 : I agree that there should be a Scottish Parliament
: I do not agree that there should be a Scottish Parliament

Q2 : I agree that a Scottish Parliament should have tax powers
: I do not agree that a Scottish Parliament should have tax powers

	Q1		Q2		%		Q1		Q2		%
	YES%	No%	YES%	No%	Turnout		YES%	No%	YES%	No%	Turnout
Aberdeen	**71.8**	28.2	**60.3**	39.7	**53.7**	Inverclyde	**78.0**	22.0	**67.2**	32.8	**60.4**
Aberdeenshire	**63.9**	36.1	**52.3**	47.7	**57.0**	Midlothian	**79.9**	20.1	**67.7**	32.3	**65.1**
Angus	**64.7**	35.3	**53.4**	46.6	**60.2**	Moray	**67.2**	32.8	**52.7**	47.3	**57.8**
Argyll and Bute	**67.3**	32.7	**57.0**	43.0	**65.0**	North Aryshire	**76.3**	23.7	**65.7**	34.3	**63.4**
Clackmannanshire	**80.0**	20.0	**68.7**	31.3	**66.1**	North Lanarkshire	**82.6**	17.4	**72.2**	27.8	**60.8**
Dumfries & Galloway	**60.7**	39.3	**48.8**	51.2	**63.4**	Orkney	**57.3**	42.7	**47.4**	52.6	**53.5**
Dundee	**76.0**	24.0	**65.5**	34.5	**55.7**	Perthshire & Kinross	**61.7**	38.3	**51.3**	48.7	**63.1**
East Ayrshire	**81.1**	18.2	**70.5**	29.5	**64.8**	Renfrewshire	**79.0**	21.0	**63.6**	36.4	**62.8**
East Dunbartonshire	**69.8**	30.2	**59.1**	40.9	**72.7**	Scottish Borders	**62.8**	37.2	**50.7**	49.3	**64.8**
East Lothian	**74.2**	25.8	**62.7**	37.3	**65.0**	Shetland	**62.4**	37.6	**51.6**	48.4	**51.5**
East Renfrewshire	**61.7**	38.3	**51.6**	48.4	**68.2**	South Ayrshire	**66.9**	33.1	**56.2**	43.8	**66.7**
Edinburgh	**71.9**	28.1	**62.0**	38.0	**60.1**	South Lanarkshire	**77.8**	22.2	**67.6**	32.4	**63.1**
Falkirk	**80.0**	20.0	**69.2**	30.8	**63.7**	Stirling	**68.5**	31.5	**58.9**	41.1	**65.8**
Fife	**76.1**	23.9	**64.7**	35.5	**60.7**	West Dunbartonshire	**84.7**	15.3	**74.7**	25.3	**63.7**
Glasgow	**83.6**	16.4	**75.0**	25.0	**51.6**	Western Isles	**79.4**	20.6	**68.4**	31.6	**55.8**
Highland	**72.6**	27.4	**62.0**	38.0	**60.3**	West Lothian	**79.6**	20.4	**67.3**	32.7	**62.8**
						SCOTLAND	**74.3**	25.7	**63.5**	36.5	**60.4**

TOTAL VOTING FIGURES

Q1, Scottish Parliament:
Yes 1,775,045 (74.29%)
No 614,400 (25.71%)

Q2, Tax-varying powers:
Yes 1,512,889 (63.48%)
No 870,263 (36.52%)

Difference between two Yes votes: 10.81%
Electorate 3,971,945; Turnout 2,389,445 (60.16%)

HOW THEY VOTED IN THE 1997 SCOTTISH DEVOLUTION REFERENDUM
SOURCE: *DAILY TELEGRAPH*, 13 SEPTEMBER

2 *On issues concerned with an alteration of the method by which Parliament is elected.*
   - The Labour government announced on 1 December 1997 that 'an alternative to the present system for parliamentary elections' would be put before the people in a referendum.

3 *Where a referendum is necessary so that the policy in question can secure legitimacy.*
   - A referendum has been proposed in Northern Ireland for any political settlement there. The Northern Ireland (Entry into Negotiations) Act 1996 provides for a referendum in relation to the outcome of all-party negotiations.

4 *Where opinion in the country does not follow party lines.*
   - In 1975, Labour Prime Minister Harold Wilson said the issue of whether to remain in the European Community on the terms renegotiated was 'one on which strong views have long been held which cross party lines'.

Local referendums

Since 1961 there have been seven-yearly referendums on the Sunday opening of public houses in the counties of Wales. These are triggered on a district-by-district basis once 500 local electors have signed a petition.

Under an obscure section of local-government legislation, six signatures of electors and 10 votes of electors at a public meeting is enough to demand a referendum. For example, in 1995, a referendum was held in East Grinstead, a town of fewer than 20,000 voters, on whether the local authority should press ahead with plans to build a community arts centre on an old school site.

HOW SHOULD THEIR USE BE REGULATED?

Simple Majority or Qualified Majority Referendums?

The Scotland Act and the Wales Act of 1978 incorporated the proviso that 40 per cent of the Scottish and Welsh electorate would have to support the devolution measures in referendums if they were to come into effect. In the Welsh referendum of 1979, devolution was defeated by a four to one majority. There was a simple majority in Scotland, 33 per cent of the electorate voting for devolution and 31 per cent against. However, it clearly fell short of the 40 per cent requirement which Parliament had imposed. The Scotland Act as well as the Wales Act was repealed by the incoming Conservative government under Margaret Thatcher.

A simple majority of the votes cast was sufficient for the devolution referendums in 1997.

The Commission on the Conduct of Referendums, jointly appointed by the Electoral Reform Society and the Constitution Unit, declared in its report published in 1996 that 'a simply majority of those who cast their votes carries a natural authority'. However, it also declared that the use of qualified majorities to approve constitutional amendments provides 'a safeguard against changing the basic laws too easily' (Report of the Commission on the Conduct of Referendums, Constitution Unit, 1996, paragraph 94).

Where it is decided to use a qualified majority, it is by no means clear that a proportion of the total registered electorate is the proper criterion to use. The electoral register is notoriously inaccurate, as the problem of implementing the 40 per cent requirement in the Scottish devolution referendum of 1979 showed. The government deducted from the total numbers on the register those not legally entitled to vote. This included voters who reached the qualifying age after the date of the referendum and voters who had died since being registered, double-registered students, student nurses, and prisoners. The government, however, was not legally allowed to make any additional discount for those in practice unable to vote, for example hospital patients or the seriously disabled. Nor was it able to take account of the likelihood of errors in the register, assumed to be around 6 per cent. Together, these deductions would have amounted to around 14 per cent of those on the electoral register. For this reason, it would be better, according to Bogdanor, if a qualified majority is desired, for this to be specified in terms of a proportion of those voting rather than of the electorate, for example 55 per cent of those voting rather than 40 per cent of the electorate.

Advisory or Mandatory Referendums?

The government was required in 1979 to lay an order before Parliament repealing the Scotland Act as well as the Wales Act. However, that repeal order could have been voted down by Parliament. The referendum was advisory. Parliament accepted an amendment proposing a mandatory referendum during the passage of the Scotland and Wales Bill in February 1977. The precedent thus created was, however, never tested as the government shortly afterwards announced that the referendum would be advisory after all and the bill was in any case withdrawn shortly after that.

Although Parliament has accepted that a mandatory referendum is possible, it seems unwise, according to Bogdanor, not to allow Parliament to look at the position again after the votes have been counted, to guard against absurdities.

Post-legislative or Pre-legislative Referendums?

The devolution referendums in 1997 were held not, as in 1979, after the legislation had been passed by Parliament, but before it was introduced. White Papers were published setting out the details of the government's plans. There were parliamentary debates, too, so that voters could acquaint themselves with the main principles of devolution on which they were being asked to vote in the referendums. The proposed referendum on electoral reform is, like that on devolution, to precede legislation, not to follow it.

Tony Blair described the purpose of the pre-legislative referendum on devolution, to prove to MPs that there was a strong demand for devolution so that they would not seek to defeat it, as a 'principled, tactical reason' for holding a pre-legislative referendum (Interview with Tony Blair, *New Statesman*, 5 July 1996). Alternatively, if the referendums were to show that there was little support for devolution, much Parliamentary time could be saved.

A post-legislative referendum allows the people to act as a check to hasty legislation or legislation which has been ill thought out.

Multi-option or One option Referendums?

Blair's government announced in 1997 the establishment of an independent Commission chaired by Lord Jenkins to recommend an alternative to the present electoral system. This would be put before the people in the Government's referendum.

The defect in this approach is that the alternative put to the voters would be one which suited the political professionals and not necessarily the one which the voters might themselves prefer.

A multi-option referendum could take many forms.

- A referendum offering the present electoral system and a number of alternatives.
- Two referendums separated by a period of time, so allowing for debate upon the possible alternatives
- A single referendum with two questions, the first asking whether voters wished to retain the first-past-the-post electoral system, the second asking which of a number of specified alternatives they preferred.

One possible model for consulting the people on electoral reform in Britain might be the two referendums in New Zealand on electoral reform, held in 1992 and 1993. New Zealand has a system of government similar to that of Britain; of all the world's political systems it is the one which approximates most closely to the Westminster model.

The first referendum put two questions to the voters, the first asking whether they favoured retention of the first-past-the-post electoral system, the second asking which of four specified alternatives they favoured. Voters were allowed to vote on the second question even if they answered 'No' to the first question, that is even if they wanted the first-past-the-post electoral system to remain.

The government indicated that the referendum would be consultative but that, if the first-past-the-post electoral system were to be rejected, it would hold a second, binding, referendum with just one question asking voters whether they preferred the first-past-the-post electoral system to the most favoured alternative in the first referendum.

In 1992 the result of the first referendum was a vote of only 15 per cent for the first-past-the-post electoral system and 85 per cent for change. The vote on the second question was 70 per cent for the mixed-member proportional system, the German system of proportional representation.

A second, binding referendum was accordingly held in 1993, setting the first-past-the-post electoral system against the mixed-member proportional system. The outcome of this referendum was that 46 per cent voted for retention of the first-past-the-post electoral system and 54 per cent for the mixed-member proportional system. This system was therefore adopted for New Zealand, and the first election under it was held in 1996.

The problem with multi-option referendums is that, as with qualified majority referendums, the question of what is to count as a legitimate outcome becomes controversial.

OTHER INSTRUMENTS OF DIRECT DEMOCRACY

Citizens' juries

A form of direct democracy has also survived in modern states in the practice of selecting juries on the basis of lot or rota – in the way (as we saw) that public offices were filled in Ancient Athens.

The experience of juries has been applied to the political process in the USA, where *citizens' juries* have been used to test political decisions against *informed and considered* public opinion. These are small groups of up to 25 individuals, drawn randomly from the electoral register, or chosen to represent a cross-section of society. Citizens' juries are brought together for about a week and given one or more questions to address. They receive information, hear evidence and cross-examine witnesses, and may call for additional data. Citizens juries discuss the matter in question between themselves, with a moderator to ensure fair play, and then draw conclusions. In the USA they have been conducted by the independent Jefferson Centre for New Democratic Processes, a Minneapolis-based foundation promoting new forms of democratic participation. In Britain, the Institute for Public Policy Research has also explored these initiatives and suggested that something similar be tried in this country (see the reference at the end of the book). One example of the spread of the jury idea was the Science Museum's UK consensus conference on plant biotechnology, held in November 1994. A 16-strong 'lay-panel' including a nurse, a caterer, an airline pilot and a roadsweeper, considered the risks and benefits of plant biotechnology, making recommendations to government.

The world's first *deliberative poll* (on crime) was imported into Britain in 1994, pioneered in the USA by James S. Fishkin (see the reference at the end of the book, and the photo). Fishkin was academic adviser to the project, sponsored by

Channel Four and *The Independent*. It was unlike any survey or poll ever conducted. Ordinary opinion polls model what the public is thinking, even though the public may not be thinking very much, or paying much attention. Deliberative polls, by contrast, model what the public *would* think if it had a better opportunity to think about the questions at issue.

A national random sample of the electorate is taken and transported from all over the country to a single place. It is then immersed in the questions at issue, with carefully balanced briefing materials, intensive discussion in small groups, and questions to competing experts and politicians. At the end of that process, the participants are surveyed in detail. The result represents the conclusions people would reach if they were better informed and had a better opportunity to think through the issues.

A CROSS-SECTION OF THE DELIBERATIVE POLLING AUDIENCE

This method tackles the two main problems which afflict the 'poll-driven, sound-bitten version of televised democracy', namely the 'rational ignorance' of ordinary citizens and the tendency of polls to report 'non-attitudes' or pseudo-opinions (see below).

As Downs argued in the 1950s, it is rational for individual citizens to avoid investing a lot of effort in becoming less ignorant. If a citizen has one vote in millions, why should he or she spend a lot of time and effort sorting through complex public policy options? A citizen's individual vote, his or her individual opinion, will not make much difference. However, if a citizen is one of a few hundred in a nationally televised deliberative poll, he or she has a real incentive to invest a lot of time and effort in attempting to understand the issues. A citizen now has the opportunity to make those opinions count, by conveying them to television viewers and to people in power.

Research has established that many of the opinions reported by polls are 'non-attitudes' or pseudo-opinions. Respondents are asked questions about which they have no knowledge and no settled views. To avoid appearing foolish, they then choose one of the options offered. In effect, they make up an opinion on the spot. The random variability of these opinions over time is one of the clues to the lack of thought on the part of the respondents.

Yet these pseudo-opinions are reported solemnly as if they were firm and settled, and as the poll results are disseminated, they then take on a life of their own. Television and polling together operate as a kind of echo chamber. Poll results are broadcast, citizens have vague impressions of the results and they then bounce them back in additional polls. Very little thinking is going on anywhere in this process.

The aim of the deliberative poll is to insert a real voice of the people, their considered judgement, into the echo chamber offered by the media. It could bring power to the people by giving the public a voice, not an echo.

Electronic democracy

Developments in communications technology have made possible other innovations in direct democracy. Some of these methods (such as QUBE) have been considered by Demos, an independent think-tank (see the reference at the end of the book). Since the mid-1970s, experiments in the USA and elsewhere have tested the potential of *electronic democracy*. For example, local leaders debated issues, while viewers periodically registered agreement or disagreement, on the 'QUBE' cable system in Columbus, Ohio. Another method was Santa Monica's Public Electronic Network (PEN). Citizens using home computers or terminals in public locations could access information, complete transactions, send email to officials or representatives, and participate in computer conferences on issues of concern.

Cable operators are the key players for developing new ideas for electronic democracy.

Limitations

Instruments of direct democracy such as citizens' juries and electronic referendums might help to take power away from the political class, transferring it to the people.

However, the basic limitation of attempts to involve citizens in government through citizens' juries or electronic referendums is that, while they may involve citizens in some high-profile decisions and may involve the public in consultation on the formulation of policies, they cannot superintend the regular workings of modern large-scale government. Furthermore, electronic democracy is likely to be only partially inclusive, leaving many citizens uninvolved and uncomprehending, especially those who currently under-participate in politics. The problem would be especially acute if these quick fixes were added to the present highly centralised state, for it could just as likely enhance the power of the governors over the governed as it would increase democratic input. It could supplement government power with electronic legitimacy, enabling politicians to mobilise consent on certain key issues while leaving others unaddressed.

THE BRITISH SYSTEM AS LIBERAL DEMOCRATIC

The British system of government possesses few external constraints and relatively weak internal constraints.

EXTERNAL CONSTRAINTS

- It is a system of government according to prescribed rules which imposes limits on the government, but has no written constitution enforceable in the courts.
- Civil liberties are protected to some extent, but there is no strong bill of rights. The Human Rights Bill, 1997, incorporating the European Convention on Human Rights into British law, addressed criticism from some quarters that the idea of incorporation would interfere with the sovereignty of Parliament. While judges would be able to declare past or future Acts of Parliament 'incompatible' with the Convention, they would not, like a Supreme Court, be able to strike them down. Instead, ministers would be expected to amend the conflicting law by a new, fast-track procedure, subject to parliamentary approval.
- Things are done according to law, but Parliament, in practice the government, has unrestricted discretionary power.
- Voluntary organisations play an important part in the British system. However, they cannot prosper where there is a tendency to centralise power, with the government then pressing them to become more bureaucratic and managerial, more externally accountable and less internally accountable.

INTERNAL CONSTRAINTS

- The British system of government is fragmented to some extent, with checks and balances, but the system of parliamentary government allows little room for a separation of powers.

- Bicameralism is weak in that the House of Lords has little legislative power.
- There is decentralisation of government power, notably to Scotland, but without the relinquishment of sovereignty, the British Constitution remains unitary rather than federal.

DEMOCRATIC MATTERS

The British system of government is also open to criticism on democratic grounds.

- It is a form of **representative democracy**, but neither the head of state, the Monarch, nor the second chamber, the House of Lords, is elected.
- Elections are held regularly, at least once every five years (except in wartime), conducted on the basis of 'one person, one vote'. The main aim of each of the Parliamentary Boundary Commission's decisions is to create constituencies of approximately equal-size electorates. However, the first-past-the-post electoral system produces a system in which the value of a vote varies with the party supported. For example, in 1983 it took about 33,000 votes to elect a Conservative MP, 40,000 votes to elect a Labour MP, and 338,000 votes to elect an Alliance MP.
- Vote is by secret ballot but, for example, freedom of expression is limited by unequal access to the mass media.
- The electorate has a choice between rival candidates advocating to some extent rival policies, but political power is concentrated in the hands of a ruling elite in Parliament and government. Quangos, quasi-autonomous non-governmental organisations, have been given central roles in the provision of services and the regulation of activities that might have been assigned to, or remained with, more accountable public institutions. For example, Urban Development Corporations have extensive discretionary powers, are independent of local authorities, and are not accountable to local residents.

HOW CAN DEMOCRATIC ACCOUNTABILITY BE ENHANCED?

According to Paul Hirst, the current essential task is to simplify government and devolve its powers so that the existing institutions of representative democracy can begin to function somewhat as they were intended to do in the nineteenth century. The aim must be to simplify the core institutions of government and the role of legislation without reducing the public services or welfare provisions that are essential to a well-managed modern industrial society.

According to Hirst, the solution here lies in the restructuring of the state and the redrawing of the relationship between the public and the private spheres. This involves three distinct but complementary strategies of reform:

1 *Decentralisation, devolving powers to elected regional governments with legislative and fiscal powers* (authority to influence economic activity by manipulating the levels and allocation of taxes and spending). Comparative evidence demonstrates that regional governments are likely to have more effective local knowledge than do central governments. They are able to promote consent and involvement, through dialogue with local representative bodies such as trade associations and unions, in areas like collective services to industries or local education and training.
   Regional governments are large enough entities to take over effectively many of the functions of economic regulation, social provision and planning currently performed by central government. They could take over the responsibility for rendering key quangos like Urban Development Corporations and Training Enterprise Councils more accountable. If they acquire major functions of central government, then they are also likely to attract the attention of voters. Because they are bigger and more diverse, they are less likely to become dominated by a single party, especially if they are elected by means of proportional representation. As regional governments will be of some consequence, they are also more likely, than are local authorities, to attract high-quality politicians.
2 *The devolution of functions to self-governing voluntary associations, and assistance to them via grants from public funds proportional to size of membership.* The advantage of promoting the performance of governmental and public functions by voluntary associations is that they both reduce the administrative load on government institutions and can be directly accountable to their members, thus increasing the decentralisation of democratic supervision.
   A radical shift in this direction would simplify the tasks of government, reducing its performance of two contradictory roles: that of service provider and that of overseeing the services provided.
3 *The democratisation of quangos*. Directly to democratise many quangos like NHS Trusts, higher-education corporations, locally-managed schools, and Housing Action Trusts so as to involve both their personnel and their consumers in many of their boards of management, would serve to return these institutions to those involved in them, rather than having them controlled by nominees who often do not use the services in question or know little about them.

According to Hirst, 'publicising' civil society, by creating forms of democratic self-governance under the general superintendence of representative institutions, is a better solution than managerialising it and reducing the involvement of citizens in their services and institutions. This redrawing of the boundary between public and private, accepting democracy in civil society, also enables us to see a way of simplifying the scale and scope of legislation. If citizens are responsible for making their own rules for those activities of direct concern to them, then legislation need deal with fewer possible future events or conditions and guard directly against fewer risks and abuses. It can concentrate on protecting citizens from a more limited range of harms, and can act as a means of appeal rather than as an initial-remedy provider or all-purpose source of regulation.

SUMMARY

The British type of democracy is liberal democratic.

Its distinctive features are the liberal element of limited government and the democratic element of popular consent.

Principal criticisms of liberal democracy have been elitism, marxism, and radical emphasis on the need for participation by the people.

The British system possesses few external and relatively weak internal constraints upon government. It is also open to criticism on democratic grounds.

Revision Hints

Make sure you understand the term democracy and can distinguish between types of democracy. In particular, you should know the distinctive features of liberal democracy.

You should be able to explain the elitist, Marxist and radical criticisms of liberal democracy. Make sure you can distinguish between a referendum and an initiative. You should be able to argue the case for and the case against referendums and initiatives, as well as considering the questions of when referendums should be held and how their use should be regulated.

Make sure you can evaluate how accurate it is to describe the British political systems as liberal democratic.

Exam Hints

Answering short questions on 'British Democracy in Context'

1 (a) Describe two types of democracy.
(b) Outline two criticisms of democracy in Britain.

The Mark Schemes and Examiner's Reports are reproduced from the London Board Edexcel, Government and Politics Advanced Level Paper 1, June 1997, with permission from London Examinations, A division of Edexcel Foundation. (Edexcel Foundation, London Examinations accepts no responsibility whatsoever for the accuracy or method of working in the answers given.)

Mark Scheme

	SCHEME	MARKS
Level 1	Poor or very limited attempt to answer one or both parts of the question. Vague description of the term democracy.	0-6
Level 2	Basic but limited attempt to answer one or both parts of the question. Some understanding shown of the term 'democracy', some attempt to describe different types and mention of criticism eg electoral system.	7-12
Level 3	Both parts attempted. Adequate to sound understanding of the term 'democracy'. The response will clearly indicate different types and their definition. One or two criticisms of democracy in Britain outlined.	13-19
Level 4	Very good to excellent account; both parts well answered. Clear description of two types of democracy given, ie. direct or representative, liberal. Good evidence of evaluative skills shown through the use of examples. Examples given of criticism of British democracy...	20-25

Examiners' Report

The Examiners' Report stated that the best candidates 'were able to make distinctions between different types of democracy, the most favoured being direct and representative'. In part (b) 'the electoral system and the growth of the executive and non-accountable bodies were the most popular criticisms.'

Note that some theories of democracy do not lend themselves to a meaningful comparison, such as democratic elitism which is, in a sense, a theory about how liberal democracy works.

2 (a) Define constitutionalism.

(b) Outline two ways in which the British system might be regarded as departing from this concept.

Examiners' Report

The Examiners' Report commented: "Level 1 responses made a limited attempt to answer both parts of the question but indicated little understanding of the term 'constitutionalism', often confusing the term with 'unwritten constitution'.

Level 2 responses tended to cope with part (a) quite well but found part (b) more difficult. Level 3 candidates responded to both parts of the question in an adequate manner and showed a reasonable understanding of the term 'constitutionalism'."

3 Outline (a) a case for and (b) a case against holding referendums.

Examiners' Report

The Examiners' Report commented: 'Some candidates encountered problems in attempting to show a theoretical understanding as well as using contemporary political debate'.

4 In what circumstances should referenda* be used?

Mark Scheme

	Scheme	Marks
Level 1	Poor or very limited response indicating little understanding of the term 'referenda'.	0-6
Level 2	Basic but limited understanding of the term. Some attempt to outline examples or reasons for holding referenda.	7-12
Level 3	An adequate to sound response, indicating a sound understanding of the term 'referenda'. Reasonable outline of reasons for holding referenda, ie. constitutional issues, above politics, etc.	13-19
Level 4	Very good to excellent account. Clear understanding of the term indicated. Good account relating to circumstances given...	20-25

* Either referenda or referendums is possible for the referendum in its plural manifestation. The 'Concise Oxford Dictionary of Current English' (1990) and 'The New Shorter Oxford English Dictionary' (1993) gave both forms and expressed no preference.

Practice Questions

1 a Define democracy.

b To what extent is the British system of government democratic?

2 How should the use of referendums be regulated?

5

REPRESENTATIVE AND RESPONSIBLE GOVERNMENT IN BRITAIN

Introduction

THIS CHAPTER WILL explain the idea of representative government. It will examine representative government in Britain, including the question of whether Members of Parliament should be representatives or delegates, the doctrine of the electoral mandate, the under-representation of women and ethnic minorities.

The idea of responsible government will also be explained. Responsible government in Britain will be examined, including collective responsibility and how this has been weakened; individual ministerial responsibility, limitations on its effectiveness, changes affecting its operation, levels of its operation, when ministers resign, evasion of responsibility and reforms.

Finally, the distinction between 'responsible' government in Britain and 'representative' government in the USA will be made.

Key points

- The idea of representative government, and its British features.
- The idea of responsible government, and its British aspects.
- The distinction between 'responsible' government in Britain and 'representative' government in the USA.

THE IDEA OF REPRESENTATIVE GOVERNMENT

It is generally agreed that a political system can properly be described as a system of **representative government** if it is one in which representatives of the people share, to a significant degree, in the making of political decisions.

But what is a representative of the people? This is a question to which answers vary, not in the sense that they are contradictory but in the sense that they emphasise different qualities which a representative ought to possess. A.H. Birch uses the term 'representative' in three different ways:

1. to denote an agent or delegate, that is a person whose function is to protect and if possible advance the interests of the individual or group on whose behalf he or she is acting. Salespeople, barristers and ambassadors are representatives in this sense;
2. to describe people who have been elected and who have some obligation, however slight, to advance the interests and opinions of their electors;
3. to signify that a person or a group of people mirrors the main characteristics of the public. Public-opinion pollsters use the word in this sense when they speak of a representative sample.

These three usages of the term indicate three different ways in which representatives can represent the people: by virtue of their activities, by virtue of the manner of their selection, or by virtue of their personal characteristics. To put this in another form, it can be said that the people can be represented in three alternative ways: where the representatives conceive their duty to be the protection of the people's interests; where they have been elected by the people; or where they are the same sort of people as 'the people'.

REPRESENTATIVE GOVERNMENT IN BRITAIN

REPRESENTATIVES OR DELEGATES?

The traditional view in Britain has been that Members of Parliament should be representatives in the sense of the second usage above, acting in accordance with their own judgement, rather than as delegates of their constituents as in the first usage.

This was stated very clearly in the writings of Algernon Sidney:

> *It is not therefore for Kent or Sussex, Lewes or Maidstone, but for the whole nation, that the members chosen to serve in these places are sent to serve in Parliament. And though it be fit for them ... to harken to the opinions of the electors for the information of their judgements, and to the end that what they say may be of more weight ... yet they are not strictly and properly obliged to give account of their actions to any, unless the whole body of the nation for which they serve, and who are equally concerned in their resolutions, could be assembled.*
>
> *Algernon Sidneys,* Discourses Concerning Government, *1698*

Edmund Burke, an eighteenth century political theorist, echoed the same sentiments in the well-known speech which he made to the electors of Bristol after the declaration of the poll in 1774. Parliament, he said, was

> *not a* congress *of ambassadors from different and hostile interests; which interests each must maintain, as an agent and advocate, against the other agents and advocates; but Parliament is a* deliberative *assembly of* one *nation, with* one *interest, that of the whole; where not local purposes ought to guide, but the general good, resulting from the general reason of the whole. You choose a member indeed; but when you have chosen him, he is not a member of Bristol, but he is a member of* parliament.

A representative should keep in close touch with his constituents, and should even:

> *prefer their interests to his own. But his unbiased opinion, his mature judgement, his enlightened conscience, he ought not to sacrifice to you. ... Your representative owes you, not his industry only, but his judgement; and he betrays, instead of serving you, if he sacrifices it to your opinion.*
>
> *Works, vol I, p447, Bohn's Standard Library, London 1887*

THE DOCTRINE OF THE ELECTORAL MANDATE

The doctrine of the **electoral mandate** is bound up with the first above usage of the term representative. It is the idea that a general election gives the elected government a mandate to put its policies into effect. A much more vague concept of the mandate is that the party which wins an election has 'a mandate to govern', it being understood that, unless the election happens to have been dominated by a single issue – which is an exceptional circumstance – the government should be free to pursue whatever policies it thinks appropriate. It has often been asserted that a government's 'mandate to govern' does not necessarily entitle it to introduce a major change of policy, of a kind likely to arouse political controversy, if the electors have not had the chance to express their views on the subject.

In so far as the doctrine of the mandate is based on fact, it is invalid. Voting-behaviour studies demonstrate that the majority of electors do not make up their minds on how to vote on the basis of the policies outlined in the election manifestos.

The outcome of the referendum in Wales in 1979 served to disprove the theory that a general election provides a specific mandate for a government to pursue the policies outlined in its election manifesto. Welsh devolution had been supported by three of the four parties competing in Wales, the Labour Party, the Liberal Party and Plaid Cymru, parties which together gained 75 per cent of the votes cast in the October 1974 General Election preceding the referendum. However, only one in five Welsh voters could be found to endorse Welsh devolution.

UNDER-REPRESENTATION OF WOMEN AND ETHNIC MINORITIES

Critics who suggest that the House of Commons would be improved if it were a social microcosm of the people are using the term representative in the third above sense.

For example, the House of Commons became more representative of women after the General Election of 1997 than ever before. 119 women were elected as Members of Parliament, the highest ever number of female MPs. This number is nearly twice the total of 62 women elected at the General Election of 1992.

However, there are still only 18 per cent female MPs after the 1997 General Election (see the pie chart opposite). This compares with over one-third of women MPs in Germany, Sweden, Norway and Finland. The comparatively high number of female Labour MPs after the 1997 General Election (see the bar graph opposite) could be attributed to the party's policy of having women-only shortlists of prospective parliamentary candidates for winnable seats. This controversial policy was declared illegal and was abandoned a few months after being introduced (by which time some candidates had already been selected).

Tony Blair said at the Labour Party Conference in 1997:

We cannot be a beacon to the world unless the talents of all the people shine through. Not one black high court judge; not one black chief constable or one black army officer above the rank of colonel. Not one Asian either. Not a record of pride for the British establishment. And not a record of pride for Parliament that there are so few black and Asian MPs.

- There were only nine MPs from ethnic-minorities in the House of Commons after the 1997 General Election, out of 659.
- In the top five grades of the Civil Service, there were only 58 people from ethnic-minorities out of over 3,000 Whitehall policy-makers (see the bar graphs, p 56).

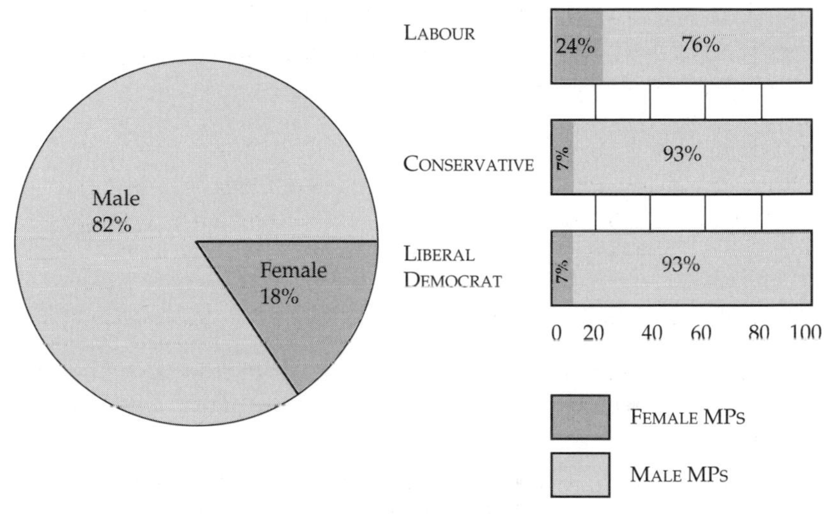

Percentage of female MPs after the 1997 General Election

Percentage of female MPs in the three major parties after the 1997 General Election

Source: Politics Review, Vol 7, no. 1

- Every judge at the highest level was white; there were four non-white circuit judges, out of a total 556.
- The most senior black policemen in Britain were both superintendents, none chief constables.
- The Army, too, was far from representative of the nation it sought to defend. There were 315 ethnic-minority officers in the UK regular forces – just 0.97 per cent of the total, compared to 6 per cent of the total workforce who came from the ethnic minorities.

THE IDEA OF RESPONSIBLE GOVERNMENT

Like the idea of representative government, that of responsible government is somewhat ambiguous. Birch uses the concept in three quite distinct ways:

1 to describe a system of government in which the government is responsive to public demands and movements of opinion;
2 to invoke the concepts of duty and moral responsibility. The ministers in office are responsible for seeing that the government pursues a wise and consistent policy, whether or not what they do meets with the immediate approval of the public.

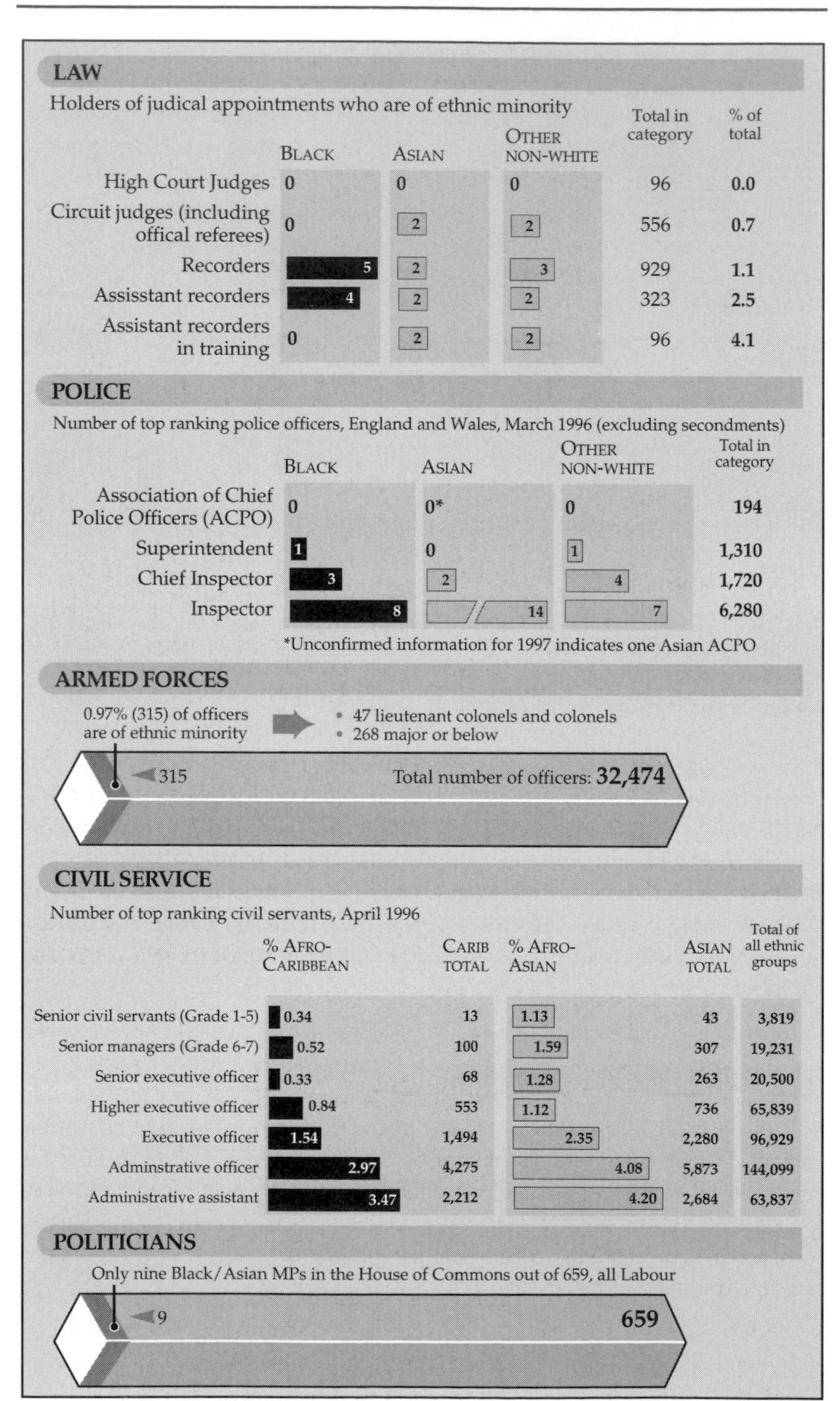

LAW

Holders of judical appointments who are of ethnic minority

	Black	Asian	Other non-white	Total in category	% of total
High Court Judges	0	0	0	96	0.0
Circuit judges (including offical referees)	0	2	2	556	0.7
Recorders	5	2	3	929	1.1
Assisstant recorders	4	2	2	323	2.5
Assistant recorders in training	0	2	2	96	4.1

POLICE

Number of top ranking police officers, England and Wales, March 1996 (excluding secondments)

	Black	Asian	Other non-white	Total in category
Association of Chief Police Officers (ACPO)	0	0*	0	194
Superintendent	1	0	1	1,310
Chief Inspector	3	2	4	1,720
Inspector	8	14	7	6,280

*Unconfirmed information for 1997 indicates one Asian ACPO

ARMED FORCES

CIVIL SERVICE

Number of top ranking civil servants, April 1996

	% Afro-Caribbean	Carib total	% Afro-Asian	Asian total	Total of all ethnic groups
Senior civil servants (Grade 1-5)	0.34	13	1.13	43	3,819
Senior managers (Grade 6-7)	0.52	100	1.59	307	19,231
Senior executive officer	0.33	68	1.28	263	20,500
Higher executive officer	0.84	553	1.12	736	65,839
Executive officer	1.54	1,494	2.35	2,280	96,929
Adminstrative officer	2.97	4,275	4.08	5,873	144,099
Administrative assistant	3.47	2,212	4.20	2,684	63,837

POLITICIANS

Statistics for Afro-Caribbean, Asian and other non-white personnel in public-sector services. Source: *The Guardian*, 2 October 1997.

It is clear that these two usages are not always compatible with one another. A government which is perfectly responsive to public demands and opinions would find itself pursuing policies that were certainly inconsistent and probably unwise. For example, the prevailing view might be simultaneously in favour of increasing government expenditure, reducing taxation, and securing a budget surplus. There is, in fact, an imminent conflict between the desire that governments should be responsible in the first sense of the term and the desire that they should be responsible in the second sense. This conflict constitutes one of the dilemmas which politicians of all countries have to face. Different political systems have different arrangements for dealing with this dilemma.

3 to signify the accountability of ministers, or of the government as a whole, to an elected assembly.

RESPONSIBLE GOVERNMENT IN BRITAIN

When people in Britain refer to the principle of responsible government, it is the third meaning of the term that they usually have in mind – that the government is collectively accountable to Parliament for its policies, while individual ministers are accountable for the work of their departments.

COLLECTIVE RESPONSIBILITY

According to convention, ministers must uphold the principle of **collective responsibility**. Decisions reached by the Cabinet or Cabinet committees are binding on all members of the government. Collective responsibility requires that ministers should be able to express their views frankly in the expectation that they can argue freely in private while maintaining a united front when decisions have been reached. This in turn requires that the privacy of opinions expressed in Cabinet and Cabinet committees should be maintained.

The principle of collective responsibility imposes certain obligations on former ministers contemplating the publication of material based upon their recollections of the conduct of government business in which they took part. In such cases, they are required to submit their manuscript to the Secretary of the Cabinet. In 1976 there was an attempt by the Attorney-General to prevent the publication of the Crossman Diaries, written by Richard Crossman on the basis of his experiences as a Cabinet Minister in the 1964–70 Labour Government. Crossman's right to publish was eventually confirmed in court. Since then, there have been numerous diaries published by former Ministers.

Sir Geoffrey Howe's resignation in 1990 over Britain's role in, and relationship with, the European Union was an example of a resignation in accordance with the convention of collective responsibility. His position was then Leader of the

House and Deputy Prime Minister, and he disagreed with Prime Minister Thatcher's policy regarding Britain's role in Europe. He said that he realised that the task had become futile of 'trying to stretch the meaning of words beyond what was credible, of trying to pretend that there was a common policy'.

Parliamentary private secretaries (PPS) are not members of the government, but their special position in relation to the government means that no parliamentary private secretary who votes against the government 'may retain his or her position' (Ministerial Code, July 1997, paragraph 46). For example, three parliamentary private secretaries who voted against the Blair Labour government over cuts in lone parent benefits in 1997 did not retain their positions. Gordon Prentice, Parliamentary Private Secretary to the Transport Minister of State, and Mick Clapham, Parliamentary Private Secretary to the Health Minister of State, resigned. Alice Mahon, Parliamentary Private Secretary to the Secretary of State for Culture, was dismissed by the Prime Minister Tony Blair.

MINISTERIAL CODE – A CODE OF CONDUCT AND GUIDANCE ON PROCEDURES FOR MINISTERS

Collective responsibility

16 The internal process through which a decision has been made, or the level of Committee by which it was taken, should not be disclosed. Decisions reached by the Cabinet or Ministerial Committees are binding on all members of the Government. They are, however, normally announced and explained as the decision of the Minister concerned. On occasions it may be desirable to emphasise the importance of a decision by stating specially that it is the decision of Her Majesty's Government. This, however, is the exception rather than the rule.

17 Collective responsibility requires that Ministers should be able to express their views frankly in the expectation that they can argue freely in private while maintaining a united front when decisions have been reached. This in turn requires that the privacy of opinions expressed in Cabinet and Ministerial Committees should be maintained. Moreover Cabinet and Committee documents will often contain information which needs to be protected in the public interest. It is therefore essential that, subject to the guidelines on the disclosure of information set out in the Code of Practice on Access to Government Information, Ministers take the necessary steps to ensure that they and their staff preserve the privacy of Cabinet business and protect the security of Government documents.

18 The principle of collective responsibility and the need to safeguard national security, relations with other countries and the confidential nature of discussions between Ministers and their civil servants impose certain obligations on former Ministers who are contemplating the publication of material based upon their recollection of the conduct of Government business in which they took part. They are required to submit their manuscript to the Secretary of the Cabinet …

Cabinet Office, July 1997.

The weakening of collective responsibility

Collective responsibility has been weakened by the extent to which modern ministers have not, strictly speaking, maintained a united front when decisions have been reached in private which are binding on all members of the government. They have seemed willing, and often able, to make speeches or write newspaper articles which clearly reveal their disagreements with particular aspects of government policy. For example, as Cabinet Minister, Michael Portillo made a number of speeches which seemed to indicate his dissatisfaction with certain policies of the Major government, but he retained his position in the Cabinet due to the support he enjoyed on the Thatcherite Right of the Conservative Party.

A second way in which collective responsibility would appear to have been weakened somewhat concerns the way it has, on three occasions this century, been suspended due to deep divisions within the government over a major issue of policy:

1. The so-called 'agreement to differ' of 1932 arose out of disagreements between ministers of Ramsay MacDonald's National (coalition) Government over import duties. The Cabinet had found it impossible to reach a unanimous conclusion on the recommendations of a Cabinet committee. However, 'with the paramount importance of maintaining national unity' in the presence of the grave problems confronting the country, it determined that 'some modification of usual Ministerial practice' was required. Ministers who found themselves unable to support the conclusions arrived at by the majority of their colleagues were at liberty to express their views by speech and vote.
2. In 1975, the Prime Minister, Harold Wilson, claimed that the 1932 precedent was a 'sound' one after his statement in the House of Commons that those ministers who did not agree with the government's recommendation in favour of continued membership of the European Community were free to advocate a different view during the referendum campaign of the country. The circumstances of the referendum were unique. Freedom to advocate a different view did not extend to parliamentary proceedings and official business.
3. The third 'agreement to differ' was in 1977 over the method of election to the European Parliament, which was to be directly elected for the first time in 1979. The issue was whether to use the first-past-the-post system or some form of proportional representation. The Prime Minister, Jim Callaghan allowed a free vote on the European Assemblies Bill, whereby ministers were permitted to vote how they wished, rather than adhere to any official Cabinet line. When questioned about the status of the convention of collective responsibility, Callaghan's response was that it still applied 'except in cases I announce that it does not'.

In 1997 Tony Blair indicated that there would be an 'agreement to differ' on the Labour Party's proposed referendum on electoral reform.

Another manifestation of the weakening of collective responsibility has been the increasing trend for former ministers to publish their memoirs, some of which have contained a considerable amount of material about confidential discussions between ministers. For example, a few days after his resignation as Chancellor of the Exchequer in 1989, Nigel Lawson had few qualms about revealing his version of discussions with Mrs Thatcher which were so confidential that he had requested that no official note-takers be present.

It is clear, therefore, that in effect the convention of collective responsibility is increasingly invoked, or not invoked, for political ends rather than as a constitutional principle.

INDIVIDUAL MINISTERIAL RESPONSIBILITY

According to the convention of **individual ministerial responsibility**, ministers have a fundamental duty to account to Parliament. This has, essentially, two meanings.

First, that the executive is obliged to give an account: to provide full information about, and to explain, its actions in Parliament so that they are subject to proper democratic scrutiny. This obligation is central to the proper functioning of Parliament, and therefore any minister who has been found to have knowingly misled Parliament should resign. While it is through ministers that the government is properly accountable, the obligation to provide full information and to explain the actions of government to Parliament means that ministers should allow civil servants to give an account to Parliament through select committees when appropriate – particularly where ministers have formally delegated functions to them, for example in the case of chief executives of executive agencies.

Second, a minister's duty to account to Parliament means that the executive is liable to be held to account: it must respond to concerns and criticism raised in Parliament about its actions because Members of Parliament are democratically-elected representatives of the people. A ministers' effective performance of his or her functions depends on having the confidence of the House of Commons (or the House of Lords for those ministers who sit in the upper House).

MINISTERIAL CODE

> Ministers have a duty to Parliament to account, and be held to account, for the policies, decisions and actions of their Departments and Next Steps Agencies;
>
> It is of paramount importance that Ministers give accurate and truthful information to Parliament, correcting any inadvertent error at the earliest opportunity. Ministers who knowingly mislead Parliament will be expected to offer their resignation to the Prime Minister;
>
> Ministers should be as open as possible with Parliament and the public, refusing to provide information only when disclosure would not be in the public interest, which

should be decided in accordance with relevant statute and the Government's Code of Practice and Access to Government Information (Second Edition, January 1997);

Similarly, Ministers should require civil servants who give evidence before Parliamentary Committees on their behalf and under their directions to be as helpful as possible in providing accurate, truthful and full information in accordance with the duties and responsibilities of civil servants as set out in the Civil Service Code (January 1996).

Ministerial Code, July 1997, paragraph 1 (ii) to (iv), repeating requirements Parliament has itself laid down, set by a Resolution carried on 19 March 1997.

See pp 64–5 for a discussion on Next Steps Agencies.

Limitations on the effectiveness of individual ministerial responsibility

By the twentieth century, there were developments which made such a convention a questionable means for securing government accountability:

- *the decline of Parliamentary power*: this was directly linked to the increasing importance of the electorate, as the prime source of government power, and to the development of the party system. After the passage of the 1867 Reform Act, the role of the House of Commons began to change. Its main purpose became to support the elected government and to pass its legislation. Acting as a check on the executive became a function of the Opposition, and was thus of limited effectiveness as the whips imposed strict party discipline. The priorities of the House therefore changed: it acted firstly as a legislative machine and only secondly as a check upon the executive.
- *the increased functions of government*: just as the start of Parliament's decline can be dated from the nineteenth century, so the acceptance that the state should have an extended role can also be attributed to this time. The growth in the size and diversity of departments was already making it impossible for a minister to be personally aware of all that was happening in his or her name, and this trend continued.

CHANGES AFFECTING THE OPERATION OF INDIVIDUAL MINISTERIAL RESPONSIBILITY

Recent changes within Parliament and government have affected the operation and level of accountability required:

The post-1979 departmentally-related select committees

A new system of departmentally-related select committees of the House of Commons was established in 1979. These committees are appointed to examine the expenditure, administration and policy of principal government departments and associated public bodies over which there is a significant degree of ultimate ministerial accountability. Norman St. John-Stevas, the then Leader of the House of Commons, said 'The objective of the new Committee structure will be to strengthen the accountability of Ministers to the House for the discharge of their responsibilities.' They have powers 'to send for persons, papers and records' relevant to their terms of reference. These powers can be exercised, formally, by the issue of an order for an individual to attend or to provide evidence. Enforcement of these formal powers is retained by the House of Commons itself and can be exercised only by the House as a whole, not by the select committee.

- The provision of evidence by civil servants to select committees
  The central principle in the provision of evidence by civil servants to select committees is that it is their duty 'to be as helpful as possible' (see the Cabinet Office reference at the end of the text, commonly known, after its original draftsman, as the Osmotherly Rules). They should be as forthcoming as they can in providing information, whether in writing or in oral evidence, relevant to a select committee's field of inquiry. Any withholding of information should be limited to reservations that are necessary in the public interest.
  However, there are limitations to this helpfulness, mainly based on the role of civil servants.
- The role of civil servants giving evidence to select committees
  Civil servants who give evidence to select committees do so on behalf of their ministers and under their directions.
  This is in accordance with the principle that it is ministers who are directly accountable to Parliament both for their own policies and for the actions of their departments. Civil servants are accountable to ministers and are subject to their instruction; but they are not directly accountable to Parliament in the same way. This does not mean, of course, that civil servants may not be called upon to give a full account of government policies, or indeed of their own actions or recollections of particular events, but their purpose in doing so is to contribute to the cental process of ministerial accountability, not to offer personal views or judgements on matters of political controversy.

DISCUSSION OF GOVERNMENT POLICY

Officials should as far as possible confine their evidence to questions of fact and explanation relating to government policies and actions. They should be ready to explain what those policies are; the justification and objectives of those policies as the Government sees them; the extent to which those objectives have been met; and also to explain how administrative factors may have affected both the choice of policy measures and the manner of their implementation. Any comment by officials on government policies and actions should always be consistent with the principle of civil service political impartiality. Officials should as far as possible avoid being drawn into discussion of the merits of alternative policies where this is politically contentious. If official witnesses are pressed by the Committee to go beyond these

limits, they should suggest that the questioning should be referred to Ministers.
A Select Committee may invite specialist (as opposed to administrative) officials to comment on the professional or technical issues underlying government policies or decisions. This can require careful handling where Committees wish to take evidence from, for example, government economists or statisticians on issues which bear on controversial policy questions and which are also matters of controversy within the respective profession. Such specialists may find themselves in some difficulty if their own judgement on the professional issues has, or appears to have, implications that are critical of Government policies. It is not generally open to such witnesses to describe or comment upon the advice which they have given to Departments, or would give if asked. They should not therefore go beyond explaining the reasoning which, in the Government's judgement, supports its policy. The status of such evidence should, if necessary, be made clear to the Committee. If pressed for a professional judgement on the question the witness should, if necessary, refer to the political nature of the issue and, as above, suggest that the line of questioning be referred to Ministers.

Departmental Evidence and Response to Select Committees Cabinet Office, 1997, paragraphs 48–49.

Nor is it the purpose of civil servants to become involved in what would amount to disciplinary investigations which are for departments to undertake.

- The conduct of individual civil servants

Civil servants should also not become involved in their own conduct or the conduct of another named civil servant.

Questions from a select committee may appear to be directed to the conduct of individual civil servants, not just in the sense of establishing the facts about what occurred in making decisions or implementing government policies, but also with the implication of allocating individual criticism or blame. In such circumstances, and in accordance with the principle of ministerial accountability, it is for the minister to look into the matter and if necessary to institute a formal inquiry. It is then the minister's responsibility to inform the committee of what has happened and of what has been done both to put the matter right and to prevent a recurrence.

If it is foreseen that a select committee's line of enquiry may involve questions about the conduct of named civil servants, it should be suggested to the committee that it would be appropriate for a minister or a senior civil servant designated by the minister to give evidence, rather than the named civil servants in question. If a civil servant giving evidence to a committee is unexpectedly asked questions which are directed at his or her individual conduct, or at the conduct of another named civil servant, the civil servant should seek instructions from ministers, and the committee should be asked to allow time for this (see again the Cabinet Office reference at the end of the book).

- The summoning of named civil servants
  The government has been reluctant to accept the power of select committees to summon named civil servants. By the same principle of ministerial accountability, it is customary for ministers to decide which civil servant or civil servants should represent them. Select committees have generally accepted this position.
  Where a select committee indicates that it wishes to take evidence from a particular named civil servant, ministers retain the right to suggest an alternative civil servant to that named by the committee if they feel that the former is better placed to represent them. While the committee is under no obligation to accept the minister's proposal, it is open to the minister to appear personally before the committee in the unlikely event of their being no agreement about which civil servant should most appropriately give evidence. If a committee nonetheless insists on a particular civil servant appearing before it, contrary to the minister's wishes, the formal position remains that it could issue an order for attendance, and request the House of Commons to enforce it. In such an event (so far unprecedented) the civil servant, as any other citizen, would have to appear before the committee but, in all circumstances, would remain subject to ministerial instruction. This would seem a definite recognition of the right of select committees to order a named civil servant to attend, but there is the implication that the government would concede this right only reluctantly and if it is formally exercised.

Next Steps Agencies

Next Steps Agencies were established following the Ibbs Report of 1988 on *Improving Management in Government: The Next Steps*. This recommended that:

> *As far as is practicable, the executive functions of Government, that is service delivery undertaken by departments (as distinct from policy), should be carried out by executive units clearly designated within departments, referred to as agencies, with responsibility for day to day operations delegated to a chief executive responsible for management within policy objectives and to a resources framework set by the responsible minister.*

Next Steps Agencies are located within government departments and staffed by civil servants. They operate under framework agreements which delegate authority and responsibilities to the chief executive who is then accountable to the minister.

Where a select committee wishes to take evidence on matters assigned to an agency in its framework document, ministers normally wish to nominate the chief executive as the civil servant best placed to represent them. While agency chief executives have managerial authority to the extent set out in their framework documents, like other civil servants they give evidence on behalf of the minister to whom they are accountable and are subject to that ministers's instruction.

Next Steps Agencies raise particular problems for accountability. These include:

1 the danger that the separation of policy and operations will be used by government to evade accountability;
2 the possibility that chief executives will be held blameworthy for agency failings in which the minister has played a part;
3 a concern that agencies will 'de-politicise the functions of government', so that accountability will focus almost exclusively on operational issues (i.e. the chief executive's responsibilities) and ignore policy and resourcing (the minister's responsibilities);
4 the uncertainty surrounding accountability when public services and functions are contracted out.

LEVELS OF OPERATION OF INDIVIDUAL MINISTERIAL RESPONSIBILITY

The accountability constitutionally required varies depending on the degree of control exercised by the minister. Where there is no ability to control, there is no requirement of accountability.

Thereafter, the obligation that individual ministerial responsibility lays on the minister in terms of accounting to Parliament varies according to the extent of his or her responsibilities, that is according to whether the minister has a direct or indirect responsibility and to what other arrangements there may be for accountability. The obligation ranges from what Diana Woodhouse calls redirecting and reporting through explanatory and amendatory action to resignation, thus producing a scale of accountability. Not surprisingly, the requirements of accountability are more frequently satisfied at the lower than at the higher end of the scale.

Redirectory responsibility

This is the starting point for accountability. The requirement here is simply for the minister to 'redirect' questions from Members of Parliament as appropriate. Such redirection applies to areas of government from which the minister is deliberately distanced, for example decisions involving individual taxation or immigration appeals. Increasingly important within this category are matters which fall within the responsibility of the chief executives of Next Steps Agencies. However, here the minister retains direct responsibility, and thus an MP can still insist upon a ministerial reply.

Moreover, because the minister is directly responsible, the replies of the chief executives are published in *Hansard*, the daily Official Record of Parliamentary proceedings, and are thus open to public scrutiny as well as to scrutiny by MPs. This makes it less easy for accountability to be 'lost' between the minister and chief executive, with both disclaiming responsibility.

Redirection concerns mostly written questions or oral questions requiring routine information or explanation. It is not meant to be a mechanism for the redirection of politically sensitive issues away from the Parliamentary arena. Such questions still demand a ministerial answer.

Reporting or informatory responsibility

The second level of ministerial responsibility requires the minister simply to report to Parliament what has happened in one of the areas of his or her responsibility. The minister will frequently preface his or her statement with 'I have been advised by the Chairman ...' or 'The Chairman has told me ...'. Such remarks indicate that the minister's responsibility is confined to acting as a mechanism for the indirect accountability to Parliament of the organisation concerned, and thus the extent to which he or she can answer questions is limited.

Informatory responsibility is improper when the advising agent is a departmental civil servant. However, ministers are known to use the associated phraseology in an attempt to distance themselves from an incident concerning their department or to abdicate responsibility on the grounds that they were 'advised' by their civil servants to take a certain course of action. This has arisen particularly in relation to legal advice, where on occasions ministers have appeared to abdicate responsibility on the basis of legal advice received, the implication being that it was the legal adviser not the minister who was at fault.

Similarly, there is a danger that ministers will limit their role with regard to executive agencies to one of simply repeating what they have been told by chief executives. This too is improper as ministers retain a direct responsibility to the House of Commons and thus are subject to the higher levels of responsibility. They are required to give full explanations for the operation and policies of their agencies. This may encourage ministerial interference in agencies which are politically controversial and thus undermine the delegated responsibility of the chief executive. However, such a possibility should result not in the acceptance of reduced accountability to the House but rather in a determination to improve the structure of accountability so that instances of ministerial interference are made public along with other information relating to agency performance.

Explanatory responsibility

The third level of responsibility requires ministers to explain or account for their own and their departments' actions. It is unacceptable for a minister to accept responsibility but to refuse to explain what has happened. Responsibility and explanation go hand in hand as part of the same process.

Explanatory responsibility is at the centre of a minister's accountability to Parliament. Moreover, since the reform of the select committee system in 1979, it has become increasingly important, involving departmental civil servants and, more recently, the chief executives of Next Steps Agencies, as well as ministers, in the accounting process.

Executive agencies offer the prospect of improved accountability because of their transparency (clarity about who can be held responsible) and management structure. However, they may still present problems either of evasion, when the extent of ministerial involvement is at issue, or of confused accountability, when it is not clear where responsibility lies. This is likely to remain a problem as long as responsibility, on the one hand, is delegated to chief executives but accountability to select committees, on the other hand, is not.

Amendatory responsibility

At the fourth level ministers are required to provide more than an explanation of what has happened. They are required to make amends for their own or their departments' shortcomings. At its simplest, an apology to the House of Commons may suffice, particularly if coupled with the announcement that corrective action has been taken. This may involve the installation of new procedures to prevent a repeat of the incident, the holding of an internal inquiry, or the disciplining of the civil servant responsible. When the incident has had serious consequences, then some kind of financial compensation may be appropriate, as with the collapse of the investment management company, Barlow Clowes. An external inquiry may be necessary as an initial step. Prison escapes are usually followed by such an inquiry, as are major prison disturbances. Exceptionally, the appropriate first step in the amendatory process will be the setting up of a public inquiry, as for example with the Scott Inquiry in 1993 after the collapse of the Matrix Churchill prosecution over the export of arms to Iraq.

The announcement of an inquiry suggests full fact finding and public accountability, but accountability may be limited by the terms of reference of the inquiry and the timing and extent of the publication of its reports. An inquiry can in practice be a useful device for the minister, delaying full disclosure of the facts until public interest has subsided. An inquiry is in any case only the initial step in the amendatory process. Much depends on how the minister acts upon the findings of the report.

The public disciplining of civil servants as an amendatory measure does not happen often. It is a constitutional requirement that the minister protect his or her civil servants from public scrutiny. There have, however, been examples of 'naming and blaming' which have arisen as a result of external inquiries, such as the one into the collapse of the Vehicle and General Insurance Company in 1971. These are controversial because civil servants are unable to defend themselves. 'Naming and blaming' is likely to increase with the establishment of executive agencies, where, in the cases of mismanagement or maladministration, the appropriate amendatory action may be the public disciplining of the civil servants in charge. However, as long as the conventional position remains that chief executives speak on behalf of the minister and not on their own behalf, the removal from office remains controversial and is likely to arouse charges of 'scapegoat'.

Chief executives also announce amendatory measures, but it is not always clear whether these measures are being taken on their own behalf, after consultation with the minister, or on the minister's instructions.

Sacrificial responsibility

This is the highest level of responsibility, and it requires the minister to resign. A departmental fault in which the minister was involved, or of which he or she knew or should have known, is a constitutional requirement for resignation.

WHEN DO MINISTERS RESIGN?

Resignations for a departmental fault have never been common. Whether a minister is forced to resign depends on three factors: the minister, the prime minister, and the party (in the form of the 1922 Committee in the Conservative Party, particularly the Executive of the 1922 Committee).

1 *The minister*. The evidence suggests that few ministers consider themselves morally obliged to resign as an acceptance of responsibility and in recognition of their constitutional position. However, Lord Carrington's resignation from the position of Foreign Secretary after the invasion of the Falkland Islands in 1982 was an exception. The assessment made by the Foreign Office of the likelihood of an Argentinian invasion of the Falklands was wrong. Lord Carrington took responsibility and resigned. One factor in the resignation was probably Lord Carrington's unease in Mrs Thatcher's Cabinet.
2 *The party*. Leon Brittan, Secretary of State for the Department of Trade and Industry, resigned in 1986 over the selective leak of parts of a confidential letter from the Solicitor-General, Sir Patrick Mayhew, to Michael Heseltine, Secretary of State for Defence, concerning the effects of the Westland helicopter company joining with an American company, Sikorsky, on European collaborative projects. It had become clear to him that he no longer commanded the full confidence of his colleagues. He was not by all accounts a popular minister, and had no following in the House of Commons, owing his position in Cabinet to prime ministerial patronage rather than to party support. Members of the 1922 Committee called for his resignation, and this was conveyed to Mrs Thatcher by the Chief Whip, John Wakeham, after he had been briefed by the Chairman of the Committee, Cranley Onslow. The following day Leon Brittan heard from both men of the lack of support from the party.
   The 1922 Committee was also influential in Lord Carrington's decision to resign, mentioned earlier. His meeting with it was disastrous, and he was generally disliked by backbenchers. Mrs Thatcher's loyal supporters were particularly hostile to him, mainly because of his pro-European views and his

failure to clearly align with Israel, but in addition, some had not forgiven him for the Rhodesia settlement (which brought into being the independent state of Zimbabwe under President Robert Mugabe).

3 *The Prime Minister*. Mrs Thatcher had been reluctant to accept the need for resignations. She did her utmost to dissuade Lord Carrington from this course, and it was her wish that Leon Brittan remain as member of the Cabinet.

EVASION OF RESPONSIBILITY

Constitutionally, resignations provide an important public demonstration of accountability, giving at least a symbolic illustration of the working of responsible government. However, they may contain little of substance in the way of explanation.

Leon Brittan's above-mentioned resignation was an example of accountability avoidance. The Select Committee on Defence indicated that it wished to take evidence from five named civil servants, John Mogg, John Mitchell and Colette Bowe from the Department of Trade and Industry, and Bernard Ingham and Charles Powell from the Cabinet Office. However, the Cabinet Office suggested Sir Robert Armstrong, Head of the Civil Service, to represent them. The Committee did not issue an order for attendance. In such a so-far-unprecedented event, the civil servants would have remained subject to ministerial instruction under the terms of the Osmotherly Rules, referred to on p 64 above. There were also political considerations. The failure of the Defence Committee to use its power to summon the named civil servants seemed to suggest that, even if select committees have a theoretical power to summon, the force of government opposition means that practical or political considerations are likely to prevail and prevent its operation.

When the minister appeared before the Committee, he refused point black to answer a series of questions regarding the publication of the Solicitor-General's letter to him. He was being asked about things either that he had done or that had been done in his department. His refusal to answer was, in effect, a rejection by him of his obligation to give an account to Parliament.

Brittan's resignation was instead of an explanation rather than part of the accountability process.

Accountability avoidance is not confined to resigning ministers. The range of situations in which departmental culpability (i.e. blameworthiness) attaches to a minister would seem to have diminished as ministers have sought to locate culpability elsewhere, refining the policy/administrative (or operations) divide to their advantage.

The establishment of executive agencies has given ministers the opportunity to distance themselves still further. It seems that while accounting to Parliament for the actions of executive agencies remains a ministerial function, taking responsibility for these actions passes to chief executives, with ministers distancing themselves from culpability. This presents the danger that chief executives will be taking responsibility for the minister as well as for themselves.

The prisons controversy

In 1995 the then Home Secretary Michael Howard failed to provide Parliament with information which, if known at the time, might have resulted in his being required to resign. Derek Lewis, the Director-General of the Prison Service Agency, was dismissed by Michael Howard on the basis that he was responsible for prison security and thus culpable for a number of escapes. The Director-General let it be known that the Agency had been subject to constant ministerial interference and changes in policy, but the picture was not sufficiently complete for a judgement to be made on the extent of ministerial involvement and thus responsibility. Michael Howard's Junior Minister at the time, Anne Widdecombe, later said, in the House of Common on 19 May 1997, that he had taken refuge in 'semantic prestidigitation' (juggling meaning). She posed three questions to Mr Howard:

1 'Why did he say he had not personally told Mr Lewis that Mr Marriott [*see the extract below*] should be suspended immediately, when he had?'
2 'Why did he say there was no question of overruling Mr Lewis when the question had been pursued as far as consulting the Cabinet Office and legal advisers?'
3 'Why did he say that he was giving the House a full account when he knows very well that important issues which were being discussed in the House were in fact omitted from the minutes which he laid before them as a full account?'

TRANSCRIPT AT THE HEART OF THE PRISONS CONTROVERSY

Edited highlights of Michael Howard's meeting with Derek Lewis and others on 10 January 1995, after the escape of three prisoners from Parkhurst Prison. The escape came shortly after a similar incident at Whitemoor. Mr Lewis told Mr Howard that the governor, John Marriott, had broken several rules including never making a single night visit to the prison.

DEREK LEWIS: I have concluded that the existing governor cannot continue in view of the criticisms of local management ... John Marriott will be moved to other duties pending a disciplinary inquiry.
MICHAEL HOWARD: But helping with inquiries will be compatible with suspension. (*There was a break at this point*).
MH: These are serious charges at any time. Following Whitemoor, they seem breathtaking. John Marriott cannot continue as governor. It is inconceivable that disciplinary charges will not follow. I can't conceive of a clearer case for suspension.
DL: Suspension is not required under the prison discipline code.

MH: But what you have said makes clear that the code doesn't limit the grounds on which suspension can occur to security. If the governor is ... to assist in the transitional phase at Parkhurst while the new governor is put in place, that does not amount to another job. It will be seen publicly as a fig leaf. I don't want to intervene formally.
DL: We have a vacancy in the project on personnel, appraisal and training ... it has no security implications ... the post-holder will be responsible just for dissemination of the report. It is non-executive. It can come into effect immediately so that John Marriott is not suspended.
MH: That is a matter of semantics.
RICHARD WILSON: (Home Office Permanent Secretary): Are the words "is today being removed as governor" acceptable?
DL: or tomorrow?
MH: No, no, no. I want to say "is today being removed."

The Guardian, *20 May 1997.*

The Scott Report

Another instance of accountability avoidance led to the Scott Report on the Export of Arms to Iraq and Matrix Churchill (1996). The government statements made in 1989 and 1990 about policy on defence exports to Iraq failed, in Sir Richard Scott's opinion, to discharge the obligations imposed by the constitutional principle of ministerial accountability. They failed to comply with the standard set by paragraphs 1 (ii) to (v) of the Ministerial Code (1997).

William Waldegrave, who had been a Foreign Office minister at the height of the 'Arms for Iraq' affair, knew at first hand, the facts that, in Scott's opinion, rendered the 'no change in policy' statement untrue. In his evidence to the Scott Inquiry, Waldegrave strenuously and consistently asserted his belief, in the face of a volume of, to Scott's mind, overwhelming evidence to the contrary, that policy on defence sales to Iraq had indeed remained unchanged. It was clear, in Scott's opinion, that policy on defence sales to Iraq did not remain unchanged. Scott accepted that Waldegrave did not 'have any duplicitous intention' and, at the time, regarded the relaxed interpretation, or implementation, of a guideline as a justifiable use of the flexibility believed to be inherent in the guidelines. But this situation only underlined, to Scott's mind, the 'duplicitous nature of the flexibility claimed for the guidelines'.

Scott did not accept that Sir Nicholas Lyall, the Attorney-General, 'was not personally at fault' over the preparation of the Public Interest Immunity Certificates for the Matrix Churchill Trial, in particular for failing to inform the prosecution about the reluctance of one minister, Michael Heseltine, to sign a P11 Certificate. Heseltine had taken his stand on the P11 Certificate, not as a result of any legal analysis which he was not equipped to make, but as a result of an apprehension that justice might not be done if the documents were withheld from the defendants. The issues that had been raised by Heseltine's stand did not fall into the category of mundane, routine, run-of-the-mill issues that could properly be left to be dealt with by officials in the Treasury Solicitors' Department without the Attorney-General's supervision. Such an apprehension on the part of a senior minister, charged, as is the government as a whole, with the taking of decisions regarding the maintenance of national security and the promotion of the public interest, raised very serious constitutional and legal issues as to the role of P11 Certificates in criminal cases.

Here is an exchange from the Public Services Committee Report on Ministerial Accountability and Answerability, 1995–96, between Dr Wright MP and Sir Richard Scott:

> Dr Wright: 'Did something constitutionally improper happen?'
> Sir Richard Scott: 'Yes, I think it did and I said so.'
> Dr Wright: 'Did ministers behave in ways that ministers ought constitutionally not to have behaved?'
> Sir Richard Scott: 'I have said so, yes.'
> Dr Wright: 'Was Parliament denied information that Parliament constitutionally ought to have been provided with?'
> Sir Richard Scott: 'I think so, yes.'

No ministers resigned for such constitutionally improper behaviour.

REFORMS

In May 1996, in evidence to the House of Commons Public Service Committee inquiry, and in his Blackstone Lecture on Ministerial Accountability, Scott proposed a number of reforms:

1. *a Freedom of Information Act*. The importance, if ministerial accountability is to be effective, of the provision of full and adequate information is, in Scott's opinion, self-evident. He concluded that if the account given by a minister to Parliament, whether in answering Parliamentary Questions, or in a debate, or to a select committee, withholds information on the matter under review, it is not a full account. Without the provision of full information, it is not possible for Parliament, or for that matter the public, to hold the executive fully to account. It follows, in Scott's opinion, that the withholding of information by an accountable minister should never be based on reasons of convenience or for avoidance of political embarrassment, and should always require special and strong justification.

   As Scott put it in his Report:

> *If Ministers are to be excused blame and personal criticism on the basis of the absence of personal knowledge or involvement, the corollary ought to be acceptance of the obligation to be*

forthcoming with information about the incident in question. Otherwise Parliament (and the public) will not be in a position to judge whether the absence of personal knowledge and involvement is fairly claimed or to judge on whom responsibility for what has occurred ought to be placed.

The Scott Report, *Vol 4, para K8.16*

The natural consequence of individual ministerial responsibility thus ought to be a Freedom of Information Act.

2 *a revision of the Osmotherly Rules.* Civil servants could, when something has gone wrong, give evidence to select committees on their own behalf, and not under ministers' directions, on matters of fact as distinct from policy.
Scott proposed a distinction between the formation and the application of policy:

I do not see why civil servants should not, as part of the manner in which ministers render their accounts to Parliament, give information about what they have done in the discharge of their duties, not in the formation of policy, but in the application of policy or in doing governmental acts in the course of their duty.

The Public Services Committee Report, *Vol III, Q.402*

---

3 *the appointment of a Parliamentary Commissioner for Accountability.* Another means of encouraging ministers to reveal as much as possible would be to monitor refusals of information through the appointment of a senior officer of Parliament, like the Parliamentary Commissioner for Standards whose task is to monitor MPs.
The task of a Parliamentary Commissioner for Accountability would be to inquire into the adequacy of refusals on public-interest grounds to supply information. Such an officer would need to be given free access to all government documents, and could report to Parliament at regular intervals, say twice a year.

4 *that the obligation of ministers to provide information to Parliament be put into statutory form.* If this were done, it would not be Parliament and its machinery that would have the final responsibility for enforcing the obligations: it would be the courts. The constitutional obligations, at present non-justiciable, would become justiciable. Rights would be created that it would be the duty of the courts to enforce. If the obligations of accountability are not accepted by ministers, both in principle and in practice, as binding, and are not where necessary enforced by Parliament, the remedy can only lie in reducing at least this part of our unwritten Constitution into statutory form.

CONCLUSION

Government in Britain is generally more 'responsible' than government in the USA, but less 'representative'. The difference here results from differences between the systems of government in the two countries. In the USA the arrangement, as we saw in Chapter 3, is for there to be a separation of powers between one branch of the federal government, which reflects the diversity of opinions and interests within the country, and another branch which is charged with the duty of pursuing a 'responsible' policy. On the other hand, in Britain, the arrangement is for the government, while enjoying a fair degree of independence of action, to be responsible to a body of elected representatives for what it does.

SUMMARY

'Representative' is used in three different ways: delegatory, elective and characteristic.

The traditional view in Britain has been that MPs should be representatives rather than delegates. In so far as it purports to be based on fact, the doctrine of the electoral mandate is invalid. Women and people from ethnic minorities are under-represented in the British system of government.

'Responsible' is used in three different ways: to denote responsiveness; wisdom and consistency; accountability.

The third useage of the term is more common in Britain than in most other countries, to signify the accountability of the government as a whole, or of individual ministers, to an elected assembly.

However, the convention of collective responsibility in Britain has been weakened.

The effectiveness of individual ministerial responsibility has been limited by the decline of Parliamentary power and the increased functions of government. Changes within Parliament (the post-1979 departmentally-related select committees) and government (the Next Steps agencies), have affected the operation of this convention. The level of operation ranges from redirectory and reporting or informatory responsibility through explanatory and amendatory to sacrificial responsibility. Resignations in accordance with the convention of individual ministerial responsibility are infrequent.

Government in Britain is generally more 'responsible' than government in the USA, but less 'representative'.

Revision Hints

Make sure you understand the different usages of the terms representative and responsible.

You should be able to distinguish between a representative and a delegate, to assess the validity of the electoral mandate and to illustrate the under-representation of women and ethnic minorities in the British system of government.

Make sure you can define the conventions of collective responsibility and individual ministerial responsibility. You should be able to show how they operate in practice.

Exam Hints

1 Discuss the role of an MP.

The classic statements of Algernon Sidney and Edmund Burke make a valid point about the nature of representation and the role of an MP. Should MPs be representatives or delegates? Should they act accordingly to their own judgements, or behave as delegates of their constituents?

2 (a) Define the convention of individual ministerial responsibility.
(b) How effectively has it operated in practice?

Make sure you develop the essential element of 'responsibility to' Parliament.

Do not simply say that few ministers have resigned, or restrict resignation to personal scandals, but set the possibility of resignation against such factors as the minister, the party and the prime minister. Make reference to changes in the Civil Service that have eroded the convention, notably the introduction of 'Next Steps' agencies. The non-resignation of Michael Howard in 1995 is a good example of how the introduction of 'Next Steps' agencies have eroded the convention.

Practice Questions

1 (a) Define the doctrine of the electoral mandate.
(b) Assess its validity.

2 (a) Define the convention of collective responsibility.
(b) How has it been weakened in recent years?

6

THE BRITISH PARTY SYSTEM IN CONTEXT

Introduction

THIS CHAPTER WILL define a party system, and then distinguish between different types of party system (such as one-party, two-party, multi-party and dominant party), as well as explaining the advantages and disadvantages of each system. It will assess the nature of the British party system by explaining how this has changed in the post-war period.

The nature of the British party system will be further assessed by putting it in the context of long-term trends dating back to the beginnings of a nationwide British party system. Finally, the British party system post-1997 will be analysed.

Key Points

- Definition of a party system; exploring different systems.
- The changing British party system post-1945.
- Long-term trends of the British party system.
- The British party system post-1997.

PARTY SYSTEMS

THE DEFINITION OF A PARTY SYSTEM

A **party system** is defined by G. Sartori as precisely 'the *system of interactions* resulting from inter-party competition'.

A ONE-PARTY SYSTEM

To be precise, **one-party system** is a misnomer. How can one party produce, alone, a *system*? A system of what? Surely not of parties. Hence, one party cannot produce a party system. However, the term *is* useful in distinguishing between a so-called one-party system and other party systems. The principal feature of a one-party system is that government power is invested in the hands of a single 'ruling' party whose monopoly of power is usually constitutionally guaranteed. Thus, all forms of opposition or political competition are legally prohibited. For example, in now-collapsed communist states like the Soviet Union, and in surviving ones such as China, Cuba and North Korea, 'ruling' communist parties have directed and controlled virtually all the institutions and aspects of society.

The justification for both the party's monopoly of power and its supervision of state and social institutions lies in Vanguardism, that is the belief of V.I. Lenin in the need for a party to lead and guide the proletariat (the working masses) towards the fulfilment of its revolutionary destiny. However, it has been criticised for being deeply elitist and providing the seed from which Stalinism, Joseph Stalin's brutal political discipline, grew.

A TWO-PARTY SYSTEM

According to Sartori, the conditions for a **two-party system** are:

- Two parties are in a position to compete for the absolute majority of seats.
- One of the two parties actually succeeds in winning a sufficient Parliamentary majority.
- This party is willing to govern alone.
- Alternation or rotation in power remains a creditable expectation.

The USA is an example of a state with a two-party system. Democrats and Republicans are in a position to compete for an absolute majority of seats, holding between them all the seats in Congress, that is the House of Representatives and the Senate. However, the presidential system allows one party to capture the presidency while the other controls Congress.

A two-party system presents clear choices for the voters, the majority party is able to form a government and implement its programme, and the government can then be held accountable to the voters at the next general election. It creates a bias in favour of moderation, as the two contenders for power have to battle for 'floating votes' in the centre ground.

However, critics have pointed to **adversary politics**, the argument that the swing of the electoral pendulum leads to damaging policy reversals.

A MULTI-PARTY SYSTEM

Sartori's definition of a **multi-party system** is one in which 'no party is likely to approach, or at least to maintain, an absolute majority'. For example, in Germany neither the Christian Democratic Union (CDU) nor the Social Democratic Party (SPD) have been likely to approach an absolute majority, being forced into coalitions with the small Free Democrat Party (FDP).

The strength of multi-party systems is that they create internal checks and balances within government, since the process of coalition formation and the dynamics of coalition maintenance ensure a broad responsiveness that cannot but take account of competing views and contending interests. For example, in Germany the liberal FDP exerts a moderating influence upon both the conservative CDU and the social democratic SPD.

The principal criticism of multi-party systems is that they tend to produce unstable government. For example, in Italy postwar governments have lasted on average less than a year, though **coalition government in** Germany, for example, has been stable during the same period. A more valid criticism is the over-representation of minor parties. For example, in Germany the FDP has been permanently in government.

A DOMINANT-PARTY SYSTEM

A **dominant-party system** should be distinguished from a one-party system. It is open and pluralistic, at least in the sense that a number of parties compete for power in regular and popular elections. In other words, the general public possesses the constitutional ability to remove the government from power, but chooses not to use this. A dominant-party system is, therefore, a competitive party system that tends to be dominated by a single major party which enjoys a prolonged period of government power.

Brendan O'Leary defines a dominant-party system according to four criteria:

1. A party must regularly win more seats in elections to the legislature than its opponents.
2. It must be able to stay in government on a regular basis.
3. It must govern continuously for a long time.
4. It must be ideologically dominant: it must be capable of using government to shape public policy so that the nature of the state and society over which it presides is fundamentally changed.

This definition runs into problems, however, notably in deciding how long a party must govern continuously for it to be considered 'dominant'. Three or four consecutive general-election victories? A decade or a decade and a half?

A classic example of a dominant-party system was Japan between 1955 and 1993.

- The Liberal Democratic Party regularly won more seats in elections to the House of Representatives, the lower chamber of the Japanese legislature, than its opponents.
- It was able to stay in government on a regular basis, having failed to gain an overall majority in the House of Representatives in 1976, 1979 and 1983 only.
- It governed continuously for 38 years.
- It was ideologically dominant, reflecting the powerful appeal of the party's neo-Confucian principles of duty and obligation in the still-traditional Japanese countryside, as well as the strong links it had forged with business elites.

Apart from a tendency towards stability, the dominant-party system is usually, however, seen as disadvantageous.

- *The distinction between party and state breaks down.* When power ceases to alternate, an insidious process of politicisation takes place and the distinction between party and state becomes blurred. This has been particularly evident in Japan, where the LDP's status as a 'permanent' government led to an unhealthily close relationship with the state bureaucracy. For instance, about one-quarter of the members of the upper House, the Diet, were former civil servants, creating a 'revolving door' that made political neutrality in the bureaucracy virtually impossible.
- *Dominant-party complacency.* When a party starts to regard itself as a 'permanent' government, the result can be complacency, arrogance and even corruption. For example, the course of Japanese politics has regularly been interrupted by scandals, usually involving allegations of corruption. The decline of the LDP in the 1990s was closely linked to such allegations, the most serious threats to LDP dominance resulting from events such as the Lockheed bribery scandal in 1979 which provoked the resignation and later imprisonment of Prime Minister Tamaka.
- *Weak and ineffective opposition.* When parties are no longer regarded as genuine rivals for government power, views and opinions, however well expressed, no longer carry weight and can more easily be ignored. Moreover, a prolonged period in opposition brings its own problems, including a tendency towards internal disputes and divisions, resulting from mounting frustration and the fact that the prospect of power is perhaps the best guarantee of party unity.
  For example, opposition to the LDP in Japan was weak and fragmented. The principal opposition party was the Japan Socialist Party, which split in 1960 with the formation of a breakaway, more rightwing Democratic Socialist Party, and again in 1977 with the formation of the smaller Social Democratic Federation. There were also the Japanese Communist Party and Komeito, the political wing of an 8-million strong Buddhist sect.

- *A deferential political culture.* A dominant-party system tends to have a profound but insidious influence upon the political culture. Long periods of one-party rule engender the belief that the party is the 'natural' party of government; in the popular mind the dominant party is linked with security and stability, with the 'natural' order of things. In effect, longevity appears to invest the dominant party with a 'right' to govern, a fact that tends to encourage deference, conformity and a fear of change.

THE BRITISH PARTY SYSTEM 1945–74: TWO-PARTY

- The Conservative and Labour Parties were in a position to compete for the absolute majority of seats.
- One of the two parties actually succeeded in winning a sufficient Parliamentary majority, though the Labour Party succeeded in winning a majority of only 5 in 1950 and 4 in 1964 (see Table 1). These majorities were not sufficient to avoid another election within a year in 1951, which the Labour Party lost, and within 18 months in 1966, which it won with a sufficient Parliamentary majority.

Table 1: ***Number of seats 1945–97***

YEAR	CONSERVATIVE[1]	LABOUR	THIRD PARTY[2]	OTHERS[3]
1945	213	393	12	22
1950	299	315	9	2
1951	321	295	6	3
1955	345	277	6	2
1959	365	258	6	1
1964	304	317	9	-
1966	253	363	12	2
1970	330	288	6	6
Feb. 1974	297	301	14	23
Oct. 1974	277	319	13	26
1979	339	269	11	16
1983	397	209	23	21
1987	376	229	22	23
1992	336	271	20	24
1997	165	419	46	29

1 INCLUDING ULSTER UNIONISTS 1945–70.
2 THE LIBERAL PARTY 1945–79, THE LIBERAL-SDP ALLIANCE 1983–87, THE LIBERAL DEMOCRATS 1992–97.
3 INCLUDING ULSTER UNIONISTS FEB. 1974–97.

- The winning party was willing to govern alone.
- Alternation or rotation in power remained a creditable expectation, though it was called into question after the Conservative Party won three consecutive general-election victories in 1951, 1955 and 1959. There was much discussion along the lines of 'Must Labour Lose?', the title of a book by Mark Abrams and Richard Rose published in 1960.
  However, over the period as a whole, power alternated four times, rotating from Conservative to Labour in 1945, Labour to Conservative in 1951, Conservative to Labour in 1964, and Labour to Conservative in 1970.

The two-party system was a product of the vast majority of the votes being cast for the two main parties in roughly equal proportions.

- Between 1945 and 1970 the average share of the votes cast for the two main parties combined was 91 per cent, ranging from 96.8 per cent in 1951 to 87.5 per cent in 1964 (see Table 2). This was evenly divided between the Conservative Party averaging 45 per cent and the Labour Party averaging 46 per cent.

Table 2: ***Percentage of votes cast 1945–97***

YEAR	CONSERVATIVE[1]	LABOUR	THIRD PARTY[2]	OTHERS[3]
1945	39.8	48.3	9.1	2.8
1950	43.5	46.1	9.1	1.3
1951	48.0	48.8	2.5	0.7
1955	49.7	46.4	2.7	1.2
1959	49.4	43.8	5.9	0.9
1964	43.4	44.1	11.2	1.3
1966	41.9	47.9	8.5	1.7
1970	46.4	43.0	7.5	3.1
Feb. 1974	37.8	37.1	19.3	5.8
Oct. 1974	35.8	39.2	18.3	6.7
1979	43.9	37.0	13.8	5.3
1983	42.4	27.6	25.4	4.6
1987	42.3	30.8	22.6	4.3
1992	41.9	34.4	17.8	5.9
1997	30.7	43.2	16.8	9.3

1 INCLUDING ULSTER UNIONISTS 1945–70.
2 THE LIBERAL PARTY 1945–79, THE LIBERAL-SDP ALLIANCE 1983–87, THE LIBERAL DEMOCRATS 1992–97.
3 INCLUDING ULSTER UNIONISTS FEB. 1974–97.

CLASS AND PARTISAN ALIGNMENT

The two-party system was sustained by **class** and **partisan alignment**.

- Class alignment, the alignment between social class and party choice, was clear. Peter Pulzer was entirely in the academic mainstream when he wrote: 'Class is the basis of British politics; all else is embellishment and detail'. The findings of Butler and Stokes echoed broadly those of every other opinion poll or voting study, namely that 'its pre-eminent role can hardly be questioned' (see Table 3).

Table 3: *Party support by class self-image, 1963 (%)*

	Higher managerial	Lower managerial	Supervisory non-manual	Lower non-manual	Skilled manual	Unskilled manual
Conservative	87	81	77	61	29	25
Labour	14	19	23	39	71	75

Source: D.E. Butler and D. Stokes, *Political Change in Britain*, 1969, Macmillan.

- Partisan alignment, that is voters aligning themselves with parties psychologically by thinking of themselves as party supporters, was also clear. Table 4 displays the level and strength of Labour and Conservative Party identification for each of the three elections between 1964 and 1970. The overwhelming majority, 80 to 81 per cent, of the electorate identified with one of the two governing parties, half of them 'very strongly'. The two-party system rested on a bedrock of unswerving commitment.

Table 4: *Party identification, 1964–70 (%)*

	1964	1966	1970
With party identification	92	90	89
With Conservative or Labour identification	81	80	81
'Very strong' identifiers	43	43	41
'Very strong' Conservative or Labour identifiers	40	39	40

Source: B. Sarlvik and I. Crewe, *Decade of Dealignment*, Cambridge University Press, 1983.

The two-party system was widely regarded as a jewel of the political system. It was held up as a model against which the complexities and irresponsibilities of the party systems of continental Europe and even the USA were found wanting, for example by the American political scientist, Samuel Beer. The Conservative Party adapted to the managed-economy ideology defined in postwar Britain as the orthodoxy in public policy, thus creating the postwar political consensus which lasted until 1970 at least.

However, by 1974 there was growing concern about the negative consequences of the two-party system. S.E. Finer's argument was that the swing of the electoral pendulum, particularly after 1964, had led to damaging policy reversal. For example, between 1945 and 1975 there was a change in government policy on prices and incomes every 13 months on average; between 1958 and 1974 a change in corporation tax every two years on average. An atmosphere of policy uncertainty had resulted that was harmful for the economy because sound business planning became impossible.

An alternative view was advanced by Richard Rose. He argued that the direction of the British economy was primarily influenced by what he called 'long-term secular trends independent of party' and not by the movement of parties in and out of office. Between 1957 and 1979 there was no significant difference in economic inputs such as setting the minimum lending rate and the level of public sector borrowing and public expenditure, nor in economic outcomes such as inflation, unemployment and economic growth.

The two views can be reconciled. The continuities occurred in spite of the parties' attempts while in office to pursue different policies. For example, in 1970 Ted Heath's incoming Conservative government reversed its predecessor's policies on, for example, prices and incomes controls and aid to industry. However, by 1973 it had done a U-turn, moving to a statutory prices and incomes policy and massive state intervention in industry.

THE BRITISH PARTY SYSTEM 1974–79: MULTI-PARTY

For the first since 1929 no party had an absolute majority at the General Election of February 1974 (see again Table 1). The Labour Party had an absolute majority of 3 at the General Election of October 1974, but this was not maintained beyond 1976.

The average share of the votes cast for the two main parties combined fell from 91 per cent between 1945 and 1970 to 75 per cent in the two general elections of 1974 (see again Table 2). There was a marked increase in support for the third party. The Liberal Party's share of the votes cast was nearly a fifth in the 1974 elections, higher than any previous postwar election.

Parties other than the three main parties also increased their share of the votes cast. In Northern Ireland the Ulster Unionist Party had for most of its history maintained a direct organisational link with the British Conservative (and Unionist) Party, with representatives of the Party in the House of Commons taking the Conservative Party whip. However, after the Conservative government of Ted Heath prorogued the Unionist-controlled devolved legislature at Stormont in 1972, the Ulster Unionists began to organise themselves as a distinct party in the House of Commons.

In Scotland the Scottish Nationalist Party (SNP) increased its number of seats from 1 to 7 and its share of the votes cast from 11.5 per cent to 21.9 per cent in the February 1974 General Election. The SNP further increased its number of seats to 11 and its share of the votes cast to 30.4 per cent at the October 1974 General Election, its best electoral performance ever. It came second in the share of the votes cast, higher than that of the Conservative Party, and it was menacingly second in 35 out of 41 Labour Party seats.

The Welsh nationalist party, Plaid Cymru, did not fare so well. It won two seats, its first seats at a general election, in February 1974, and gained another seat in October 1974, though it lost a small percentage of the votes cast in both elections compared to 1970.

In 1977 Henry Drucker's *Multi-Party Britain* suggested that the British party system had become multi-party in character, citing the General Elections of 1974 as evidence.

The multi-party system was a result of **class dealignment** and **partisan dealignment**.

CLASS AND PARTISAN DEALIGNMENT

The general elections of 1974 witnessed a clear weakening of class alignment. Only about half of the voters now supported their 'natural' class party (see Table 5).

Table 5: *Occupational class and party choice, 1974 (%)*

	Feb 1974		Oct 1974	
	Non-manual	Manual	Non-manual	Manual
Conservative	53	24	51	24
Labour	22	57	25	57
Liberal	25	19	24	20

Source: D. Denver, *Elections and Voting Behaviour in Britain*, 2nd ed., Harvester Wheatsheaf, 1994.

The graph shown on p 85 displays the level and strength of Labour and Conservative Party identification for each of the five general elections between 1964 and October 1974. In 10 years the portion of the electorate with a 'very strong' Labour or Conservative partisanship had dwindled from being a substantial minority (40 per cent) to being a clearly insubstantial one (24 per cent). With the passage of 10 years the staunch, automatic Labour or Conservative supporter, who could be expected to turn out without fail at every general election and whose outlook on the world was one-sidedly partisan, had become a member of a small and rapidly dwindling group.

The Lib–Lab pact of 1977–8 maintained Callaghan's Labour government in office. Jim Callaghan and the Liberal Leader, David Steel, agreed the basis on which the Liberal Party would work with the government. They set up a joint consultative committee under the chairmanship of the Leader of the House of Commons. This examined government policy and other issues prior to their coming before the House, as well as Liberal policy proposals. The existence of this committee did not commit either the government to accepting the views of the Liberal Party or the Liberal Party to supporting the government on any issue. Regular meetings between the Chancellor of the Exchequer and the Liberal Party economic spokesman took place. The 'negative' effectiveness of the pact was shown, for example, in curbing ambitions for further nationalisation and for achieving expenditure restraint.

The Lib–Lab pact was not renewed in 1978, and the Callaghan government eventually collapsed in March 1979 after it lost a vote of no-confidence in the House of Commons. However, it did last for nearly a full term.

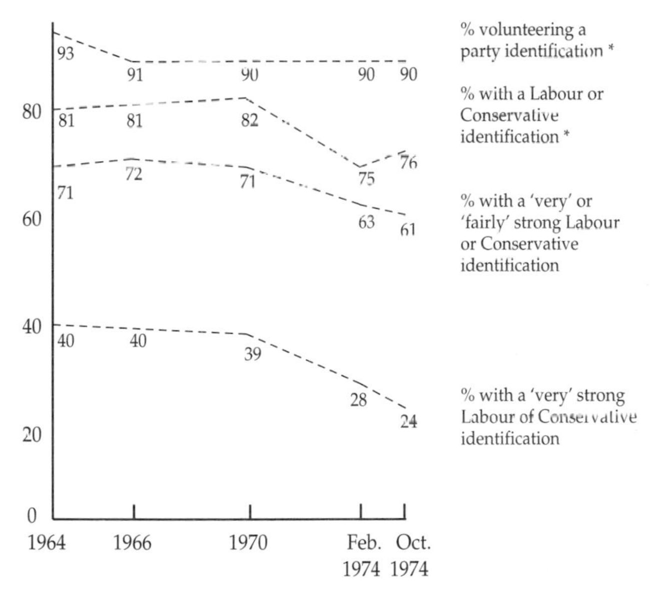

*Excludes the small number of respondents who said that they had no party identification but who subsequently said that they felt closer to one of the parties.

INCIDENCE AND STRENGTH OF LABOUR AND CONSERVATIVE PARTISANSHIP, 1964-74.
SOURCE: B. SARLVIK AND I. CREWE, *DECADE OF DEALIGNMENT*, CAMBRIDGE UNIVERSITY PRESS, 1983

'TURNING JAPANESE?' THE COVER BY JAN BROWN DESIGN FOR THE PUBLISHED LSE SYMPOSIUM OF JUNE 1992 ON BRITAIN'S DOMINANT CONSERVATIVE PARTY GOVERNMENT.

THE BRITISH PARTY SYSTEM 1979–97: DOMINANT

A symposium was held at the London School of Economics and Political Science in June 1992, organised by the LSE Public Policy Group and Common Voice, called 'Turning Japanese? Britain with a Permanent Party of Government'.

- The Conservative Party regularly won more seats in elections to the House of Commons than its opponents (see again Table 1).
- It was able to stay in government on a regular basis, with four successive election victories in 1979, 1983, 1987 and 1992.
- It governed continuously for 18 years.
- It was ideologically dominant, defining free market ideology as the orthodoxy in public policy.

Social trends seemed to be working in the Conservative Party's favour. For example, the Labour Party had been damaged by the shrinkage of the manual working class, the decline of public sector employment and consumption patterns, and the shift in the population from urban to rural areas.

However:

- In the election to the House of Commons in 1992, the Conservative Party won only 21 more seats than its opponents. This overall majority had fallen to 11 by the end of 1994, and it virtually disappeared for six months while nine Euro-sceptic rebels had the whip withdrawn (expelled from the party in Parliament). Due to by-election defeats and defections, the Party ceased to have an overall majority after the death of Barry Porter, MP for Wirral South, on 3 November 1996.

- Between 1979 and 1992 the Conservative Party's share of the votes cast was never more than 43 per cent (see again Table 2). This was not only lower than the winning party in every election between 1945 and 1966, but also lower even than the 'losing' party in 1951 and 1955. Only in 1979 was it higher, marginally, than the losing party in 1959, 1964 and 1970.
- In Scotland the Conservative Party was far from being dominant. The decline in support for the Conservative Party there accelerated sharply in the 1980s. By 1987 the Conservative Party's share of the vote in Scotland had reached an all-time low of 24 per cent. Although it increased slightly in 1992 to 25.7 per cent, it was still only just over 4 per cent more than the Scottish National Party (21.5 per cent). Its share of the vote in Scotland was down to 14.5 per cent in the 1994 European elections, much less than the 33 per cent of the SNP. In elections to the new unitary authorities in 1995, its share of the Scottish vote was only 11.3 per cent, again much less than the 29 per cent of the SNP.
- The decline in support for the Conservative Party in Wales was less pronounced. Nevertheless, Plaid Cymru had become the second party both in the 1993 county council elections, winning 41 seats compared to the Conservative Party's 32 seats, and in the 1994 European elections.
- The trend towards multi-partism in Britain as a whole continued. Between 1979 and 1997 the average share of the vote of the Conservative and Labour Parties combined was still only 75 per cent (see again Table 2).
- The Social Democratic Party (SDP) was formed in 1981 after the 'Gang of Four', Roy Jenkins, David Owen, Bill Rodgers and Shirley Williams, all ex-Labour Cabinet ministers, split from the Labour Party. The Alliance of the SDP and the Liberal Party reached over a quarter of the votes cast at the 1983 General Election, the highest third-party share of the vote since 1923, and only 2.2 per cent less than the Labour Party (see again Table 2). The Alliance share of the votes cast fell to 22.6 per cent at the 1987 General Election, but that was still higher than in any other postwar general election except 1983.
- The break up of the Alliance after the General Election of 1987 was matched by the rise of the Green Party, with 15 per cent of the votes cast for this party at the 1989 European elections.
- The third party (included the Liberal Party, 1979–81, the Alliance, 1981–87, the Liberal Democrats, 1988 to the present day) won more seats in elections to local councils, a fivefold increase from just over 1,000 in 1979 to over 5,000 in 1996. By 1997 there were more Liberal Democrat than Conservative councillors, and the Liberal Democrats controlled four times as many local authorities as the Conservative Party. No party had an absolute majority of

seats in 25 out of 45 English and Welsh county councils after the 1985 elections. This number fell to 12 out of 45 after the next county council elections in 1989, but after the 1991 local elections 108 out of 333 non-metropolitan district councils were left with no party having an absolute majority of seats. Twenty-eight county councils were left with no party having an absolute majority of seats after the local elections in 1993, higher than the number in 1985. By 1993 there were more than a quarter of local authorities in England, Wales and Scotland with no party having an absolute majority of seats, 153 out of 513. The vast majority of these were in the non-metropolitan areas.

- The Labour Party was dominant in the inner cities and in strongholds such as Doncaster.
- The nature of the state and society over which the Conservative Party presided did not seem to have been fundamentally changed. Opinion surveys provided evidence that the Conservative Party was out of step with some of the values still held by the majority of the electorate. For example, in 1992 55 per cent preferred a society which 'emphasises the social and collective provision of welfare to one where the individual is encouraged to look after himself' (King).

Table 6: *Social class and the vote, 1979–92 (%)*

	1979		1983		1987		1992	
	Non-manual (%)	Manual (%)	Non-manual (%)	Manual (%)	Non-manual (%)	Manual (%)	Non-manual (%)	Manual (%)
Conservative	55	36	51	35	49	37	49	35
Liberal/other	19	17	31	28	31	23	25	20
Labour	26	46	18	37	20	40	26	45
Non-manual Con + manual Lab as % of total vote[1]	51%		45%		44%		47%	
Odds ratio[2]	2.6		3.0		2.6		2.4	

[1]This shows the proportion of the voting on 'class lines', that is voters supporting their 'natural' class party; the figure is derived by adding the percentage of non-manual voters who support the Conservative Party and the percentage of manual voters who support the Labour Party and calculating this figure as a percentage of the total votes cast. [2] This is the ratio of the odds of a non-manual worker voting Conservative rather than Labour to the odds of a manual worker voting Labour rather than Conservative; see Heath, A., Jowell, R. and Curtice, J. (1985) *How Britain Votes*, Pergamon Press.

Sources: Harris/ITN exit polls, 3 May 1979, 9 June 1983, 11 June 1987, 9 April 1992.

- The traditional class basis of the vote continued to weaken. Between 1979 and 1992 the proportion voting on class lines declined from 51 per cent to 47 per cent. Among non-manual workers the Conservative Party lead over the Labour Party declined from 29 per cent to 23 per cent, a 3 per cent swing to the Labour Party (see Table 6). Two social classes in particular moved away from their 'natural' party. The professional and managerial classes (the 'ABs') swung away from the Conservative Party (down 9 per cent since 1979), mainly to the third party. Skilled manual workers (the 'C2s') swung away from the Labour Party (down 4 per cent since 1979), also to the third party.

- Table 7 shows the trends in party identification from 1974. The first row of the table show that most voters did still identify with parties. More significant is the continued decline in the proportion whose commitment to the Labour or Conservative parties was 'very strong', which is shown in the fourth row of the table. The percentage fell to only 16 per cent in 1987, and in 1992 it remained at the lowest level recorded pre-1987.

Table 7: *Trends in party identification (%)*

	1979	1983	1987	1992
With party identification	85	86	86	94
With Conservative or Labour identification	74	67	67	78
'Very strong' identifiers	21	20	19	19
'Very strong' Conservative or Labour identifiers	19	18	16	18

SOURCE: FIGURES FOR 1979 ARE FROM SARLVIK AND CREWE (1983) *DECADE OF DEALIGNMENT*, CAMBRIDGE UNIVERSITY PRESS; THOSE FROM 1983 TO 1992 HAVE BEEN CALCULATED DIRECTLY FROM THE RELEVANT BES SURVEY DATA.

CONSEQUENCES OF THE DOMINANT-PARTY SYSTEM

The relationship between the party and the state

It could be argued that an alternation in power in Britain is all the more crucial in view of the absence of the usual liberal democratic constraints upon government (see Chapter 4). Britain's highly centralised system of government means that, once elected, governments inherit enormous power, including the ability to reshape the state system itself. This was evident after 1979 in a series of profound changes that took place in the Civil Service.

Furthermore, crucial areas of public life in Britain were reformed and remodelled as a result of prolonged Conservative rule. This particularly affected health, education and training, where policy was placed in the hands of a growing number of quangos. One of the areas of concern in relation to quangos was, in the words of the 1994 Nolan Committee on Standards in Public Life, 'the process by which members and senior officers are appointed, and its impartiality'. However, there has been considerable concern about the impartiality of quangos.

For example, the five non-executive members of the board of the Dartford and Gravesend NHS Trust who 'represented' the public included the wife of the Conservative MP for Dartford, a Conservative Councillor in Sevenoaks, the Conservative leader of Dartford District Council and the Chairwoman of the local Conservative Association.

The dominant party

Conservative Party dominance began with the challenge to social democratic values that were deeply rooted in the British state and in the Conservative Party itself. Early battles between the '**wets**' and the '**drys**' were meaningful confrontations, provoking debate about both policy and ideological direction. By the end of the 18 years in power, however, free market principles stood virtually unchallenged within the party.

The existence of seldom-questioned ideological goals also meant that policy mistakes were more likely to occur. The most spectacular example of this was the ease with which Margaret Thatcher was able to gain Cabinet and Parliamentary approval for the Poll Tax (a flat rate local tax paid by virtually all adults with the idea of making councillors financially accountable to them).

Although the Conservative Party was not afflicted by Japanese-style corruption scandals, its image was tarnished by 'sleaze'. The issue of 'cash for questions', where some Conservative MPs were accepting cash for asking Questions in the House of Commons, led to the setting up of the Nolan Committee on Standards in Public Life in 1994.

The quality of the opposition parties

Conservative dominance of the House of Commons during the 1980s was not simply a consequence of its large majorities but also a reflection of the weakness of opposition parties, particularly the weak performance of the Labour Party and the division in the Opposition between the Labour Party and the Alliance, later the Liberal Democrats.

The political culture

A desire for security and familiarity, 'sticking with nurse for fear of something worse', was certainly relevant to the outcome of the 1992 General Election which the Conservative Party won at the height of a recession.

LONG-TERM TRENDS

The traditional view was that Britain had a two-party system. The scope of Robert McKenzie's study of British political parties was indicated by its subtitle, The Distribution of Power within the Conservative and Labour Parties, with the Liberal Party being relegated to an appendix. Ivor Jennings wrote that there was a 'natural' tendency for Britain to follow the two-party system; and that the 'swing of the pendulum' was a familiar feature of British politics. (See p 91.)

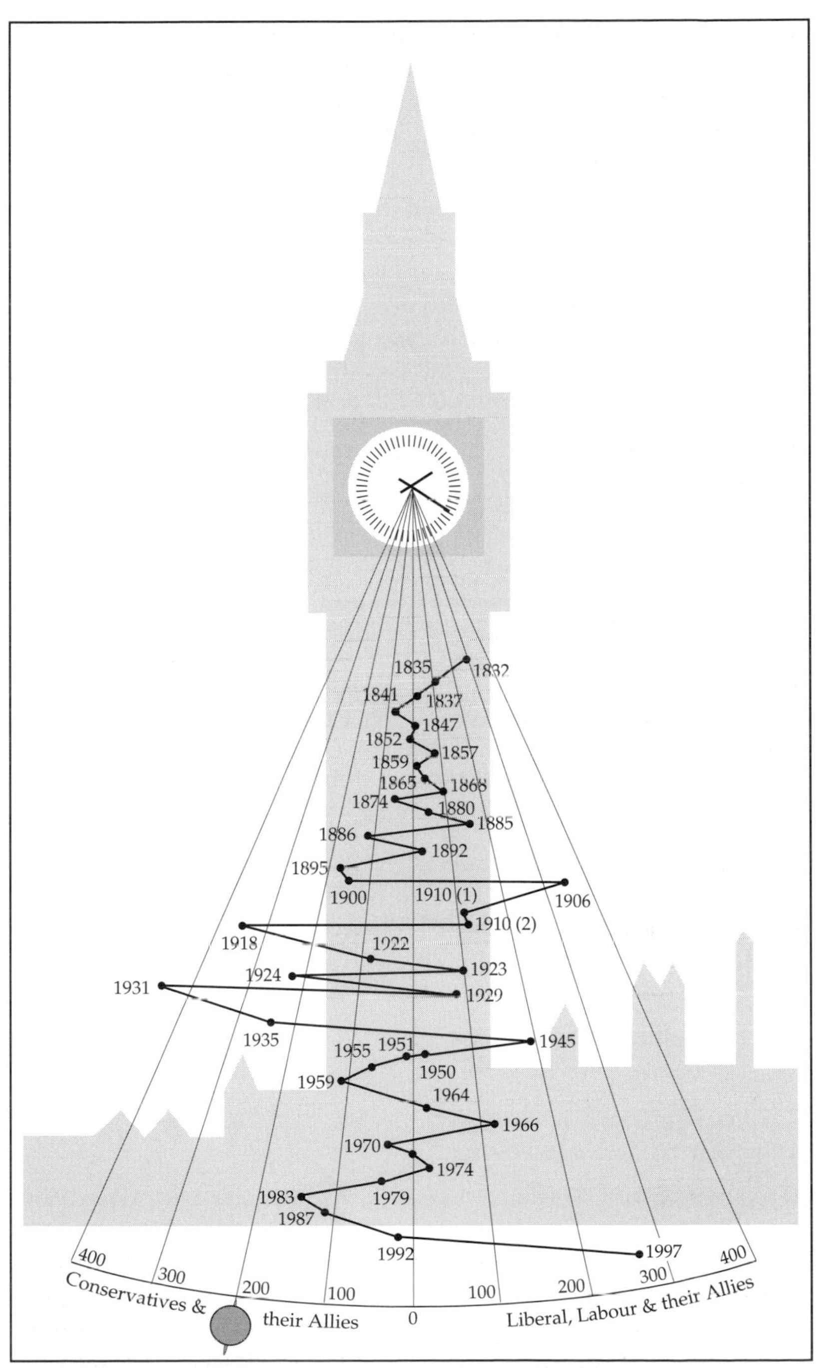

THE SWING OF THE PENDULUM: GOVERNMENT MAJORITIES FROM 1832 TO 1997. ADAPTED FROM IVOR JENNINGS, *THE BRITISH CONSTITUTION*, CAMBRIDGE UNIVERSITY PRESS, 1961

However, only since 1885 has it been appropriate to speak of a nationwide British party system, and since then it has been clearly a two-party system for only about 30 years (1945–74).

- Between 1885 and 1918 the two parties in a position to compete for the absolute majority of seats were the Conservative and Liberal Parties. One of these two parties actually succeeded in winning a sufficient parliamentary majority in only six out of eight general elections. The Liberal Party in the general elections of January 1910 and December 1910 did not win a sufficient Parliamentary majority. It continued in office as a **minority government** until 1915, when a coalition government was formed. Neither of the two parties was able to govern alone during this period, the Conservative Party needing the support of the Liberal Unionists while the Liberal Party relied on the Irish Nationalists.
- Between 1918 and 1945 the two parties in a position to compete for the absolute majority of seats were the Conservative and Labour Parties. One of the two parties actually succeeded in winning a sufficient Parliamentary majority only in 1924, the Conservative Party able to govern alone for a full term until 1929.

CONSERVATIVE DOMINANCE

The Conservative Party has been able to stay in government on a regular basis, either alone or as the dominant member of a coalition, for two-thirds of the twentieth century. Even during the period of the two-party system, 1945–74, it governed for nearly 60 per cent of the time, or nearly half as many years again as the Labour Party.

The Labour Party has succeeded in winning a sufficient Parliamentary majority to govern alone for a full term only three times, in 1945, 1966 and 1997. It has not managed to serve two consecutive full terms in office.

THE BRITISH PARTY SYSTEM POST-1997

'Is Conservatism Dead?' asked John Gray and David Willetts in a book published after the General Election in 1997.

- The result of the 1997 General Election was a disaster for the Conservative Party. Its number of seats, 165, was its lowest since the Liberal Party landslide majority of 1906, only just managing to beat that previous record low of 157 seats. The Conservative Party's share of the votes cast was lower than in any general election since 1832.
- The Labour Party succeeded in winning a landslide Parliamentary majority of 179, the biggest in postwar British politics, bigger even than the landslide of

1945 (see again Table 1). It won more seats than it had ever done before. The 10.3 per cent swing from Conservative to Labour was the largest two-party shift since 1945, almost double the previous postwar record of 5.3 per cent, in 1979. However, the Labour Party's share of the votes cast was lower than in all elections from 1945 to 1966 (see again Table 2). This was not only lower than when it won with big majorities in 1945 and 1966 but also lower than when it won only narrowly in 1950 and 1964, and lower even than when it lost in 1951, 1955 and 1959. It was only marginally higher than when it lost in 1970. At 71.2 per cent the turnout (the percentage of the electorate who voted) was the lowest in postwar elections. It was much lower in strong Labour areas than in strong Conservative ones. The Labour Party share of the electorate, that is of those registered to vote, was only 30.9 per cent. Since 1945 only those governments which emerged after the two 1974 general elections secured the active support of a lower proportion of the electorate.

- The share of the vote of the Conservative and Labour Parties combined was 74 per cent, lower than in the 1974 general elections (see again Table 2).
- The third party won 46 seats, the largest number since 1929, twice as many as the Alliance secured in 1983 (see again Table 1).
  Its share of the votes cast declined slightly, by 1 per cent, for the third consecutive election, the third party's second lowest share since 1974 (see again Table 2). However, it was still significantly higher than at any postwar election pre-1974.
- Parties other than the two main parties won 75 seats (see again Table 1), the highest since 1923. The share of the votes cast for candidates other than those from the three main parties was 9.3 per cent, the highest ever.

Table 8: *Vote and social grade in the 1997 General Election*

VOTE	SOCIAL GRADE			
	AB %	C1 %	C2 %	DE %
Conservative Change from 1992	42 (–15)	26 (–15)	25 (–13)	21 (–16)
Labour Change from 1992	31 (+11)	47 (+14)	54 (+13)	61 (+14)
Liberal Democrat Change from 1992	21 (0)	19 (–5)	14 (–4)	13 (–2)

Figures in brackets show change since 1992.

SOURCES: NOP/BBC EXIT POLL, 1 MAY 1997; NOP/BBC EXIT POLL, 9 APRIL 1992.

- Table 8 shows that the level of support for the Labour Party was clearly higher among those in blue-collar or working-class occupations (social grades C2 and

DE) than it was among those in white-collar or middle-class occupations (grades AB and C1). However, the rise in support for the Labour Party compared with 1992 was more or less the same in each social grade. The differences between the social grades were largely the same in 1997 as in 1992. The General Election of 1997 appeared to have done little to disturb the relationship between class and voting.

- The Labour Party's success in securing the largest ever postwar swing would appear to confirm that the electorate had become more volatile. However, changes in the popularity of the parties should not be confused with changes in the behaviour of individuals. The NOP/BBC exit poll found that among those who claimed also to have voted in the 1992 General Election, 23 per cent indicated that the party they voted for in 1997 was different from the one they supported in 1992. This figure was just two points higher than the 21 per cent who reporting voting differently from 1987 in the 1992 BBC exit poll. Equally, the proportion claiming to have made their mind up how to vote during the election campaign was, at 42 per cent virtually identical to the proportion who gave the same answer in 1992 (41 per cent), despite the significantly greater length of the 1997 campaign. Indeed, the General Election of 1997 may if anything indicate that partisan loyalty was more important than had recently been emphasised. Table 9 shows the relationship between age and vote. Support for the Labour Party was particularly high, no less than 19 points higher than five years previously, amongst those aged 18 to 29. It was actually two points lower among the over-65s.

Table 9: *Vote and age*

	1997 VOTE % (CHANGE ON 1992 IN BRACKETS)		
	CONSERVATIVE	LABOUR	LIBERAL DEMOCRAT
First-time voters	19 (–16)	57 (+17)	18 (–3)
All 18–29	22 (–18)	57 (+19)	17 (0)
30–44	26 (–11)	49 (+12)	17 (–3)
45–64	33 (–9)	43 (+9)	18 (–2)
65+	44 (–3)	34 (–2)	16 (+2)

SOURCES: 1992 DATA ITN/HARRIS EXIT POLL; 1997 DATA BBC/NOP EXIT POLL.

- There appeared to have been more anti-Conservative tactical voting than ever before. Voters exhibited a striking tendency to opt for whichever of the two opposition parties appeared best placed to defeat the Conservative Party locally. This can be seen in Table 10 which analyses the performances of the parties according to the tactical situation which pertained before the election (but excluding those tactical constituencies where the Conservative Party started off with less than a third of the vote). The Labour Party vote rose by around three points more in those seats where the party started off second to the Conservative Party, than in those where they were already in first place. This additional vote evidently came at the expense of the Liberal Democrats whose support fell by three percentage points more where the Labour Party began in second place rather than first.

The Labour Party was up to three points worse off in seats where the Liberal Democrats started off second, while the Liberal Democrats' performance was on average a couple of points better in such seats. In contrast, the Conservative Party performance showed little variation.

Curtis and Steed estimate than as a result of tactical switching, at least 15 and maybe as many as 21 seats were won by the Labour Party from the Conservative Party; and at least 10 maybe as many as 14 seats by the Liberal Democrats from the Conservative Party.

Table 10: *Tactical voting*

	CHANGE IN % VOTING			
TACTICAL SITUTATION	CON	LAB	LIB DEM	
Lab seats; Con over 33.3%	-12.6	+9.6	-0.3	(107)
Con/Lab seats	-12.6	+13.0	-3.0	(181)
Lib Dem seats; Con over 33.3%	-10.6	+9.6	+1.6	(8)
Con/Lib Dem; Con lead under 30%	-11.8	+6.5	+1.9	(80)
Con/Lib Dem; Con lead over 30%	-13.5	+10.0	-0.8	(60)
Three-way marginals*	-11.6	+10.9	-2.3	(18)

*Three way marginals are where Con 1st, Lib Dem 2nd in 1992, but Labour within 6% of the Liberal Democrats.

SOURCE: APPENDIX 2: 'THE RESULTS ANALYSED' J.CURTICE AND M. STEED IN D. BUTLER AND D. KAVANGH, *THE BRITISH ELECTION OF 1997*, MACMILLAN

- The electoral system is now significantly biased against the Conservative Party. If the change in each party's share of the vote in each constituency had been the same as it was across the country as a whole, then the Labour Party's majority would have been 131 rather than 179 and the Liberal Democrats would have won 28 seats rather than 46. The Conservative Party won 43 seats fewer than they might otherwise have expected.

  Two factors explain why the electoral system has become so biased against the Conservative Party. Fewer votes are cast in constituencies where the Labour Party is strong than where the Conservative Party is strong. More important is the fact that the votes for the Labour Party and Liberal Democrats have become more effectively distributed, while those for the Conservative Party have become less so.

Primarily due to tactical voting, both the Labour Party and the Liberal Democrats did better in seats where they were challenging the Conservative Party and thus had something to gain, while the Conservative Party lost support more heavily where it had seats to lose.

Table 11 illustrates the degree of bias in the electoral system. Assuming a uniform swing from the 1997 result, the Conservative Party would have to be more than one per cent ahead of the Labour Party in votes simply to deny their opponents an overall majority. In order to match the Labour Party in number of seats, the Conservative Party would need to be well over six per cent ahead in votes. The Conservative Party needs to be nearly 10 points ahead of the Labour Party to secure an overall majority.

It cannot, of course, be assumed that the electoral system will remain so biased in the future. Table 11 almost undoubtedly overestimates the extent to which the Conservative Party would be disadvantaged. Some of the tactical switching between the Labour Party and the Liberal Democrats may not repeat itself at the next general election, voters no longer having the motivation to vote against an unpopular Conservative government. However, the high level of tactical voting might almost have been encouraged by the closer proximity between the Labour Party and the Liberal Democrats, and that motivation could continue.

Table 11: *Targets for the Conservatives*

Target	Swing required %	Implied vote	
		Con %	Lab %
Deny Lab a majority	7.2	38.6	37.2
Achieve equality of seats	9.8	41.2	34.6
Win a majority	11.4	42.8	33.0

Source: NOP/BBC exit poll, 1 May 1997

Conservative Party dominance in the twentieth century is not necessarily pre-ordained, a natural state of affairs reflecting the instincts of a conservative electorate. It is more likely the result of divisions among the anti-Conservative vote. Prime Minister Tony Blair and Liberal Democrat Leader Paddy Ashdown ushered in a new era of political cooperation in September 1997 by holding the first meeting in Downing Street of a joint Cabinet committee involving ministers and senior Liberal Democrats (see the photo).

Blair's unprecedented initiative in bringing the Liberal Democrats onto a Cabinet committee was clearly not a response to any immediate electoral necessity. It could be a move in a larger strategy the aim of which is the ending of Conservative domination of British politics. At the end of September 1997, Blair told the Labour Party Conference that his heroes weren't just Ernie Bevin, Nye Bevan and Clement Atlee (all Labour), they were also Keynes, Beveridge and Lloyd George (Liberals). He added: 'Division among radicals almost 100 years ago resulted in a twentieth century dominated by Conservatives. I want the twenty-first century to be the century of the radicals.'

SEPTEMBER 1997 SAW THE FIRST JOINT CABINET COMMITTEE BETWEEN THE LABOUR GOVERNMENT AND SENIOR LIBERAL DEMOCRATS.

ELECTORAL REFORM

The British party system is an artifact (an artificial product) of the first-past-the-post electoral system. On 1 December 1997 Blair's government announced the establishment of an independent commission under the chairmanship of Lord Jenkins, recently retired leader of the Liberal Democrats in the House of Lords, to produce 'any appropriate system or combination of systems in recommending an alternative to the present system for parliamentary elections'. The commission should 'observe the requirement for broad proportionality, the need for stable government, an extension of voter choice and the maintenance of a link between MPs and geographical constituencies'. The first elections in Great Britain to be held under systems of proportional representation will take place in 1999 for both the Scottish Parliament and the Welsh Assembly, as well as the European Parliament. A House of Commons elected by means of the first-past-the-post electoral system will seem increasingly anomalous.

However, Blair remained unpersuaded on the issue. Many Labour MPs elected under the present system are unlikely to behave like 'turkeys voting for Christmas'. A report by Dunleavy, Margetts and Weir on the 1997 General Election showed that the Alternative Vote would have been even less proportional than first-past-the-post, increasing the number of Labour and Liberal Democrat MPs while cutting Conservative MPs from 165 to just 110, half the number they would be entitled to under a proportional system.

Yet even electoral reform by means of the Alternative Vote or a similar system, while clearly not proportional, would make a multi-party system more likely. In the 1992 General Election the Alternative Vote would have deprived John Major of his overall majority by a single seat, according to earlier research by Dunleavy, Margetts and Weir (see Table 12). Both the proportional systems would have ushered in a period of minority or coalition government on the 1992 pattern of voting though only the Additional Member System would have left the Labour Party short of an overall majority in 1997.

Table 12: ***How Britain would have voted under alternative electoral systems***

	Cons	Lab	Lib Dem	Green	SNP/PC	N.Ireland
Actual 1992 result	336	271	20	0	7	17
Alternative Vote (AV)	325	270	30	0	9	17
Additional Member System (AMS)	268	232	116	0	18	17
Single Transferable Vote (STV)	256	250	102	6	20	17

Since the Rowntree poll was conducted only in Great Britain, we have made no attempt to assign the 17 Northern Ireland seats between parties.

Source: P. Dunleavy, H. Margetts and S. Weir, *Replaying the 1992 General Election*, The Public Policy Group, LSE, 1992

SUMMARY

The traditional view was that Britain had a two-party system, but it has been clearly a two-party system for only about 30 years (1945–74).

Its changing nature since then, with the decline of the two-party system and the emergence of a Conservative dominant-party system for nearly 20 years (1979–97), culminated in a landslide victory for the Labour Party in 1997.

The British party system is an artifact of the first-past-the-post electoral system. Electoral reform would make a multi-party system more likely.

Revision Hints

Make sure you understand the term party system and can distinguish between a one-party system, a two-party system, a multi-party system and a dominant-party system. You should be able to explain the advantages and disadvantages of each system.

Note the changing nature of the British party system.

Exam Hints

Answering essay questions on 'The British Party System in Context'

1 Explain the disadvantages of a party system that is dominated by a single party.

Do not confuse a party system that is dominated by a single party with a 'one-party system'. Use the example of Conservative governments from 1979 to 1997. Mention also dominant parties within local government.

2 Assess the nature of Britain's party system.

Make good use of past general elections.

Explain the evolutionary nature of the British party system and of class and partisan dealignment. Describe the successive Conservative wins, pointing to a dominant-party system, and compare the system to Japan. Mention the Labour landslide of May 1997.

Offer some speculation as to the post-1997 party system following the recent General Election, perhaps forecasting a future dominant-party system but this time with a Blairite Labour government and not a Thatcherite Conservative one.

Practice Questions

1 (a) Distinguish between a one-party system and a dominant-party system.
(b) How does the definition of a dominant-party system run into problems?

2 'It is too soon to say whether 1997 will be a realigning election, in which Labour becomes the new majority, and normal party of government' (D. Butler and D. Kavangah). Discuss.

GLOSSARY

Absolute majority of seats Majority of seats over all other parties.

Additional Member System A proportional system of election under which some members are elected in single member constituencies on a first-past-the-post basis. The additional members are allocated on a proportional basis.

Alternative vote An electoral system under which the voters list the candidates in single member constituencies in order of preference; candidates have to obtain an absolute majority to be elected.

Adversary politics The argument that the swing of the electoral pendulum leads to damaging policy reversals.

Bicameralism The fragmentation of legislative power by the division of legislatures into two chambers.

Bill of rights A document that provides a legal definition of the rights of individuals in the relationships between them and the state.

Civil society A range of autonomous groups, each enjoying some measure of independence from government.

Characteristic representation Representation by a group of people who mirror the main characteristics of the people.

Class alignment The alignment between social class and party choice.

Class dealignment Weakening of the alignment between social class and party choice.

Coalition government More than one party in government.

Collective responsibility Decisions reached by the Cabinet or Cabinet committees that are binding on all members of the government, who should maintain a united front in public.

Common law Judge-made law that has developed over centuries.

Constitution The rules which regulate the composition and powers of governmental institutions, and the relationships between these institutions, as well as between them and the individual citizen.

Constitutionalism A system of government according to prescribed rules which imposes limits on the government.

Conventions of the constitution Rules of the constitution which are not law.

Delegatory representation Representation by a group of people whose function it is to protect and if possible advance the interests of the people on whose behalf they are acting.

Democracy Rule by the people, or the power of the people.

Democratic rights A range of civil liberties such as freedom of expression, freedom of assembly and freedom of movement.

Devolution The delegation of central government power without the giving up of sovereignty.

Direct democracy The direct and continuous participation of citizens in the task of government.

Dominant-party system A competitive party system that tends to be dominated by a single major party enjoying a prolonged period of government power.

'Drys' Conservatives with a tendency towards neo-Liberal Conservatism.

Elective dictatorship Centralised democracy in which the government exercises a predominant influence over the other components of the system of government.

Elective representation Representation by a group of people who have been elected, involving some obligation, however slight, to advance the interests and opinions of their electors.

Electoral mandate The idea that a general election gives the elected government a mandate to put its policies into effect.

Electorate The people eligible to vote.

Elitism A belief that political power is concentrated in the hands of a few, the elite.

Executive The branch of government that 'executes', that is applies the law.

Federal constitution A constitution in which sovereignty is divided between two levels of government.

First-past-the-post electoral system An electoral system under which the candidates have to obtain more votes than the next placed candidate to be elected.

Flexible constitution A constitution that requires no special procedure for amendment.

Individual ministerial responsibility Ministers have a duty to Parliament to account, and be held to account, for the policies, decisions and actions of their departments and Next Steps Agencies

Initiative An arrangement whereby any person or group of persons may draft a proposed law or constitutional amendment and, after satisfying certain requirements of numbers and form, have it referred directly to the voters for final approval or rejection.

Impeachment Trial of an office-holder by the legislature.

Judiciary The branch of government that judges, that is adjudicates on the law.

Justiciable Enforceable by the courts.

Legislature The branch of government that legislates, that is makes law.

Liberal democracy Limited government and representative democracy.

Minority government One party in government without an absolute majority of seats.

Multi-party system A party system in which no party is likely to approach, or at least to maintain, an absolute majority.

Neo-liberal Conservatism This approach emphasises the importance of the individual and the limited role of government.

One Nation Conservatism This approach stresses the importance of community and makes a positive case for the use of public powers to promote the general interest.

One-party system Where government power is invested in the hands of a single 'ruling' party whose monopoly of power is usually constitutionally guaranteed.

Parliamentary system of government The political executive is part of the legislature, is selected by the legislature, and can be removed by the legislature if the legislature withdraws its support.

Participatory democracy Participation by the people in the task of government.

Partisan alignment Voters aligning themselves with parties psychologically by thinking of themselves as party supporters.

Partisan dealignment A weakening in the extent, and strength, of party identification, that is of voters identifying themselves as party supporters.

Party system The system of interactions resulting from inter-party competition.

Political equality One person, one vote, one value.

Political pluralism The existence of a variety of political ideas and doctrines.

Presidential system of government The political executive is not part of the legislature, but is directly elected by the electorate, and cannot be removed from office by the legislature.

Proportional representation Any electoral system which produces representation in proportion to the votes cast.

Recall The power of the people to remove an elected official before the expiry of his or her term of office.

Quangos Bodies which have a role in the process of government but are not part of a department, and are not democratically elected.

Referendum An arrangement whereby a proposed law or policy that has been approved by a legislature does not go into force until it has been approved by the voters in an election.

Representative democracy Where the people participate indirectly in government through representatives.

Representative government One in which representatives of the people share, to a significant degree, in the making of political decisions.

Rigid constitution A constitution which can only be amended by an extraordinary procedure.

Royal prerogative Powers legally left in the hands of the Crown.

Rule of Law Government should be conducted within a framework of recognised rules and principles which restrict discretionary powers.

Separation of powers The concept of the separation of legislative, executive and judicial agencies, functions and persons.

Single Transferable Vote A proportional system of election under which the voters list the candidates in multi-member constituencies in order of preference. Candidates have to reach a quota to be elected.

Social democracy Social as well as political equality.

Sovereignty of parliament Parliament has the right to make or unmake any law whatever; no person has the right to over-ride or set aside law made by Parliament.

Statute law Law made by Parliament.

Two party system A party system where two parties are in a position to compete for the absolute majority of seats; one of the two parties actually succeeds in winning a sufficient parliamentary majority which is willing to govern alone, alternation or rotation in power of the two parties remaining a credible expectation.

Unitary constitution A constitution in which all sovereignty rests with the central government.

Unwritten constitution A constitution in which major rules are not contained in one document or series of formally related documents.

'Wets' Conservatives with a tendency towards 'One Nation' Conservatism.

Whips Party managers responsible for maintaining party discipline.

Written constitution A constitution in which major rules are contained in one formal document.

FURTHER READING AND RESOURCES

BOOKS

Abrams, M. and Rose, R. (1960) *Must Labour lose?* Harmondsworth: Penguin.

Bagehot, W. (1963) *The English Constitution*, Fontana.

Ball, A.R. (1993) *Modern Politics and Government*, 5th edn, Basingstoke: Macmillan.

Beer, S. (1965) *Modern British Politics*, London: Faber.

Birch, A.H. (1964) *Representative and Responsible Government*, London: Allen & Unwin.

Bogdamor, V. (1997) Power and the People, London: Victor Gollancz.

Butler, D. and Kavanagh, D. (1997) *The British General Election of 1997*, Macmillan.

Butler, D. and Ranney, A. (eds) (1994) *Referendums Around the World*, Basingstoke: Macmillan.

Cabinet Office (1997) *Departmental Evidence and Response to Select Committees*, London: Cabinet Office.

Demos (1994) 'Lean democracy' in *Demos Quarterly*, issue 3.

Dicey, A.V. (1987) 'The referendum' a symposium in *National Review*, March 1894.

—— (1915) *Introduction to the Study of the Law of the Constitution*, 8th edn, Macmillan.

Downs, A. (1957) *An Economic Theory of Democracy*, New York: Harper and Row.

Drucker, H. M. (ed) (1979) *Multi-Party Britain*, Basingstoke: Macmillan

Dunleavy, P., Margetts, H. and Weir, S. (1997) *Making Votes Count*, Scarman Trust Enterprise.

Finer, S.E (1975) *Adversary Politics and Electoral Reform*, Wigram.

Fishkin, J. (1991) *Democracy and Deliberation: New Directions for Democratic Reform*, New Haven: Yale University Press.

Foley, M. (1993) *The rise of the British Presidency*, Manchester University Press

Gray, J. and Willetts, D. (1997) *Is Conservatism Dead?* Profile Books.

Heywood, A. (1994) *Political Ideas and Concepts: An Introduction*, Macmillan.

—— (1997) *Politics*, Macmillan

Hirst, P. (1993) *Associative Democracy*, Cambridge: Polity Press.

Hood Phillips, O. (1978) *Constitutional and Administrative Law*, 6th edn, Sweet & Maxwell

Jennings, I. (1961) *The British Constitution*, Cambridge: Cambridge University Press.

King, A. (ed) (1992) *Britain at the Polls*, Chatham House.

Locke, J. (1924) *Two Treaties of Civil Government*, Dent

Mckenzie, R. (1955) *British Political Parties*, Oxford: Heinemann.

Macpherson, C.B. (1966) *The Real World of Democracy*, Oxford: Oxford University Press.

Margetts, H. and Smyth, G. (1994) *Turning Japanese? Britain with a Permanent Party of Government*, London: Lawrence & Wishart; particularly the essay 'Britain's Japanese Question: "Is There a Dominant Party?"' by B. O'Leary.

Michels, R. (1911) *Political Parties: a Sociological Study of the Oligarchical Tendencies of Modern Democracy*, New York, Collier.

Mills, C.W. (1956) *The Power Elite*, Oxford: Oxford University Press

Montesquieu, C-L. (1949) *The Spirit of the Laws*, New York: Hafner. Translation by T. Nugent

Mosca, G. (1896) *The Ruling Class*, Maidenhead: Mcgraw-Hill.

Pareto, V. (1935) *The Mind and Society*, London: Harcount Brace.

Pulzer, P. (1967) *Political Representation and Elections in Britain*, London: Allen & Unwin.

Robins, L. Blackmore, H. and Pyper, R. (1994) *Britain's Changing Party System*, Leicester: Leicester University Press; particularly Chapter 1, 'Britain's dominant-party system', by A. Heywood.

Rokkan, S. and Urwin, D. (eds) (1982) 'Introduction: centres and peripheries in Western Europe' in *The Politics of Territorial Identity: Studies in European Regionalism*, London: Sage.

Rose, R. (1981) *Do Parties Make a Difference?* Macmillan.

Sartori, G. (1976) *Parties and Party Systems: A Framework for Analysis*, Cambridge: Cambridge University Press.

Schumpeter, J. (1942) *Capitalism, Socialism and Democracy*, London: Allen &

Unwin.

Stewart, J., Kendall, L. and Coote, A. (1994) *Citizens' Juries*, Institute for Public Policy Research.

US Information Agency *Steering the Course: Policy Making in the USA*

Vile, M.J.C. (1967) *Constitutionalism and the Separation of Powers*, Oxford: Clarendon Press.

Wade, H.W.R. (1988) *Administrative Law*, Oxford: Oxford University Press

Woodhouse, D. (1994) *Ministers and Parliament: Accountability in Theory and Practice*, Oxford: Clarendon Press.

JOURNALS

Relevant articles appear in the following journals:

Talking Politics, the Journal of the Politics Association, available from Studio 16, 1-Mex Business Park, Hamilton Road, Longsight, Manchester, M13 OPD. For example, 'Lessons from the Maastricht Debates: the Referendum we never had' by A. Batchelor, Vol. 6, No. 3.

Parliamentary Affairs, the Journal of the Hansard Society for Parliamentary Government, available from Studio 16, 1-Mex Business Park, Hamilton Road, Longsight, Manchester, M13 OPD. For example, 'Written Constitutions: Principles and Problems' by D. Oliver, Vol. 45 No. 2.

Developments in Politics, An Annual Review, available from Causeway Press, PO Box 13, Ormskirk, Lancashire L39 5HP. For example, Chapter 2, 'The Constitution', by P. Norton, in Vol. 6.

Politics Review, available from Philip Allan Publishers Ltd., Market Place, Deddington, Oxford OX5 4SE. For example, 'Women in the House of Commons', Vol. 7 No. 1.

REPORTS

Scott, R. *Report of the Inquiry into the Export of Defence Equipment and Dual-use Goods to Iraq and Related Prosecutions*, HC 115 1995-96.

The Public Services Committee Report on Ministerial Accountability and Answerability, HC 313, 1995-96.

Efficiency Unit, *Improving Management in Government*: 'The Next Steps', HMSO, 1988

CONFERENCES

One-day conferences currently organised by, for example:

Enterprise Education Conferences, 4 Princess Road, London NW1 8JJ. Tel.: 0171 483 1349.

Student Educational Conferences, Weavers Lodge, The Green, Stalham, NR12 9QA. Tel. 01692 582565/582770.

The Politics Association (see previous address). Tel.: 0161 256 3906.

Easter Revision Conferences are also provided by Student Educational Conferences and the Politics Association in London and Manchester.

PAST PAPERS, MARK SCHEMES AND EXAMINERS' REPORTS

Examining Boards publish past papers, Mark Schemes and Examiners' Reports.

INDEX

Numbers in **bold** refer to pages on which there is a definition in the glossary.